HOW TO COOK

HOW TO COOK

A SIMPLE-TO-USE ILLUSTRATED GUIDE TO KITCHEN SKILLS
AND TECHNIQUES, WITH 500 STEP-BY-STEP PHOTOGRAPHS

NORMA MACMILLAN

HERMES HOUSE

This edition is published by Hermes House, an imprint of Anness Publishing Ltd,
Hermes House, 88–89 Blackfriars Road, London SE1 8HA; tel. 020 7401 2077; fax 020 7633 9499

www.hermeshouse.com; www.annesspublishing.com

If you like the images in this book and would like to investigate using them for publishing,
promotions or advertising, please visit our website www.practicalpictures.com for more information.

Publisher: Joanna Lorenz
Senior Cookery Editor: Linda Fraser
In-house Editor: Anne Hildyard
Copy Editors: Jane Sigal and Penny David
Designers: Sheila Volpe and Sîan Keugh
Photographer: Amanda Heywood
Food Styling: Elizabeth Wolf Cohen, steps by Marilyn Forbes and Cara Hobday

The author would like to thank Jill Eggleton for her help in testing recipes.

ETHICAL TRADING POLICY
At Anness Publishing, we believe that business should be conducted in an ethical and ecologically sustainable way,
with respect for the environment and a proper regard to the replacement of the natural resources we employ.
As a publisher, we use a lot of wood pulp in high-quality paper for printing, and that wood commonly comes from spruce
trees. We are therefore currently growing more than 750,000 trees in three Scottish forest plantations: Berrymoss
(130 hectares/320 acres), West Touxhill (125 hectares/305 acres) and Deveron Forest (75 hectares/185 acres).
The forests we manage contain more than 3.5 times the number of trees employed each year in making paper
for the books we manufacture.
Because of this ongoing ecological investment programme, you, as our customer, can have the pleasure and reassurance
of knowing that a tree is being cultivated on your behalf to naturally replace the materials used to make the book
you are holding.
Our forestry programme is run in accordance with the UK Woodland Assurance Scheme (UKWAS) and will be certified
by the internationally recognized Forest Stewardship Council (FSC). The FSC is a non-government organization
dedicated to promoting responsible management of the world's forests. Certification ensures forests are managed
in an environmentally sustainable and socially responsible way. For further information about this scheme,
go to www.annesspublishing.com/trees

Previously published as *Basic Cooking*

NOTES
For all recipes, quantities are given in both metric and imperial measures and, where appropriate, in standard cups
and spoons. Follow one set of measures, but not a mixture, because they are not interchangeable.
Standard spoon and cup measures are level. 1 tsp = 5ml, 1 tbsp = 15ml, 1 cup = 250ml/8fl oz.
Australian standard tablespoons are 20ml. Australian readers should use 3 tsp in place of 1 tbsp for measuring
small quantities.
American pints are 16fl oz/2 cups. American readers should use 20fl oz/2.5 cups in place of 1 pint when measuring liquids.
Electric oven temperatures in this book are for conventional ovens. When using a fan oven, the temperature will
probably need to be reduced by about 10–20°C/20–40°F. Since ovens vary, you should check with your manufacturer's
instruction book for guidance.
Medium (US large) eggs are used unless otherwise stated.

PUBLISHER'S NOTE
Although the advice and information in this book are believed to be accurate and true at the time of going to press,
neither the authors nor the publisher can accept any legal responsibility or liability for any errors or omissions that may
have been made nor for any inaccuracies nor for any loss, harm or injury that comes about from following instructions
or advice in this book.

Contents

~

Introduction	6
Poultry & Meat	10
Fish & Seafood	30
Pasta, Grains & Pulses	46
Vegetables	58
Eggs	76
Fruit & Ices	88
Breads & Cakes	100
Pastry	114
Index	126

~ INTRODUCTION ~

Whether you are a complete novice, an experienced cook or an occasional dabbler, there are times when everyone longs for basic techniques and methods to be laid out clearly and simply. This book does just that.

In addition, there are lots of recipes and recipe ideas too, so you can try out the skills you are learning or brushing up. The recipes are designed to illustrate a particular technique. When you read these recipes, take a moment to assess any additional techniques required. Look them up in the index, if you want to review.

USEFUL EQUIPMENT

To be able to cook efficiently and with pleasure, you need good equipment. That is not to say that you should invest in an extensive and expensive collection of pots, pans, tools and gadgets, but a basic range is essential.

In addition, buy the best equipment you can afford, adding more as your budget allows. Well made equipment lasts and is a sound investment; inexpensive pans and tins are likely to dent, break or develop 'hot spots' where food will stick and burn, so will need replacing. Flimsy tools will make food preparation more time consuming and frustrating.

For the top of the stove

When choosing pots and pans, look for those with heavy bottoms, sturdy insulated handles and knobs and tight-fitting lids. Bear in mind, too, how much the pan will weigh when full – a large pot for pasta or stock must not be too heavy for you to lift.

Copper conducts heat best, but is hard to care for. Aluminium is good, as is cast iron, although the latter needs scrupulous care to prevent rust. A vitreous enamel coating on cast iron is a good compromise. Stainless steel is lightweight and durable, but it conducts heat unevenly. A composite or clad bottom containing another metal can improve heat conduction.

- **Stove top essentials:** At least 3 saucepans with lids (2, 3 and 5 pint/1, 2 and 3 litre); small and large frying pans with lids; large flameproof casserole with lid; stockpot or pasta pan with lid.
- **Helpful equipment:** Omelette pan, double saucepan, wok, pancake pan, sauté pan, ridged grill pan, steamer.

For the oven

Cake and bun tins and baking sheets should be made of shiny metal (aluminium, tin or stainless steel) for even heat distribution. Pie and flan tins should be dull metal, glass or ceramic. Roasting tins can be made of any material, but they must be sturdy.

- **Baking and roasting essentials:** 2 round sandwich tins; 8 in (20 cm) or 9 in (23 cm) round and square cake tins; large baking tin (13 × 9 in/33 × 23 cm); large and small loaf tins; deep bun tin; 9 in (23 cm) pie tin; oval or round pie dish; 9 in (23 cm) flan tin with removable bottom, or flan ring; 9 in (23 cm) springform cake tin; Swiss roll tin; 2 baking sheets; roasting tin with rack; large soufflé dish; shallow and deep baking dishes; grill pan with rack; wire rack; oven gloves; oven and meat thermometers.

- **Helpful equipment:** Sandwich tins, round and square cake tins, pie tins, flan tins, springform tins and tartlet tins in alternative sizes; individual soufflé dishes, gratin dishes, ramekins, metal skewers.

Cutting tools

A good set of knives is the most important tool in food preparation. Yet so many cooks make do with flimsy, dull or nicked knives, which can turn even the chopping of onions into an arduous task.

Knives made of carbon steel can be given the sharpest edge, but they rust and discolour easily so must be washed and dried immediately after use. High-carbon stainless steel knives will take a sharp edge and they resist discoloration, but are more expensive. Ordinary stainless steel knives are very difficult to sharpen efficiently. Whatever knives you choose, keep them sharp. More accidents occur with blunt knives than sharp ones.

- **Cutting essentials:** Chef's knife with 10 in (25 cm) blade, paring knife with 3 in (7.5 cm) blade, flexible vegetable knife with serrated edge and pointed tip, rigid serrated knife with 10–12 in (25–30 cm) blade, sturdy kitchen scissors, knife block or magnetized bar, several cutting boards in different sizes for different uses.
- **Helpful cutting tools:** Filleting knife with thin flexible 7 in (18 cm) blade and sharp point, boning knife with thin 6 in (15 cm) blade, utility knife with 6 in (15 cm) blade, grape-fruit knife with curved serrated blade, poultry shears, carving knife and fork.

Preparation tools

You can do a lot with just a big bowl and a sturdy spoon, but there are many tools that make cooking easier.

● **Preparation essentials:** 4 mixing bowls in varying sizes, wooden spoons, long-handled slotted spoon, ladle, wooden spatula, rubber spatulas in varying sizes, palette knife with flexible 10 in (25 cm) blade, fish slice, tongs, large balloon whisk, hand-held electric mixer, potato masher, lemon squeezer, colander, kitchen scales, jug and measuring spoons, vegetable peeler, grater, 2 sieves (1 metal, 1 nylon), long 2-pronged fork, rolling pin, pastry brush, can and bottle openers, corkscrew, kitchen timer, paper towels, wraps, string.

● **Helpful equipment:** Salad spinner, food processor and/or blender, potato ricer, meat mallet, rotary grater, nutmeg grater, citrus zester, canelle knife, apple corer, melon baller, pastry blender, pastry scraper, trussing needle, cherry stoner, pasta machine, table-top electric mixer, baking parchment.

BUYING AND STORING FOOD

A well-stocked kitchen makes meal preparation easy. The key is planning – planning menus for the next few days or the week ahead, then making a shopping list that includes fresh foods as well as those frequently used foods whose stocks are running low or that are near or past their use-by date. Allow yourself to be a little flexible, though. When shopping, take advantage of fresh seasonal foods and special offers.

Knowing how and where to store food – both fresh and preserved – and how long to keep it will be a great help in shopping to stock the kitchen.

In the refrigerator

All foods in the refrigerator or freezer should be well wrapped or stored in sealed containers. This preserves flavour and moisture, and prevents the flavours and odours of other, stronger foods being transferred. It is essential to keep raw meat and poultry well wrapped as their drippings can transfer bacteria to other foods.

Perishable fresh foods, such as meats, poultry, fish and seafood, eggs, cheese and other dairy products, and many fruits and vegetables must be kept refrigerated at a temperature of 35–40°F (1–5°C). For longer storage, many can also be frozen at 0°F (–18°C) or lower. Cooked leftovers must also be refrigerated or frozen. Check fridge and freezer temperatures with a special thermometer. If temperatures are too high, food will spoil rapidly.

Storing fresh fruits

Those fruits that can be kept at room temperature while still unripe include apricots, kiwi fruits, mangoes,

nectarines, papayas, peaches, pears, pineapples and plums. Once ripe, all these should be refrigerated and eaten within 2–3 days.

Fruits that can be stored at cool room temperature include apples (although they will be crisper if refrigerated), bananas, dates, grapefruit and oranges. Apples can be kept at room temperature for a few days, dates for several weeks, and grapefruit and oranges for up to a week; beyond that, refrigerate them.

Unless you intend to eat them on the day of purchase, refrigerate fully ripe and perishable fresh fruits. These include berries, cherries, figs, grapes, lemons, limes, melons, pomegranates and tangerines. They can be kept refrigerated for 2–3 days.

Storing fresh vegetables

Like fruits, there are se vegetables that can stored at room temperature. A dark, cool place (about 50°F/10°C) with good ventilation is ideal. Suitable vegetables are garlic, onions, potatoes and sweet potatoes, swede and pumpkin. All can be kept for about 2 months. Store tomatoes at room temperature until they are ripe. After that, refrigerate.

Perishable vegetables should be refrigerated. Some, such as peas or sweetcorn, should be used quickly, while others, like carrots or cabbage, can be kept for a longer period. In most cases, do not wash the vegetable until just before using. Celery, frisée, escarole, spring greens, herbs, lettuce, spinach and watercress should be washed before storage.

Storing canned and dry foods

Full cupboard shelves are a boon for a busy cook, but canned and dry foods can deteriorate if not stored properly or if left too long on the shelf. Kitchen cupboards should be cool (no more than 65°F/18°C) and dry. Staples such as flour, salt, sugar, pasta and grains are best stored in moisture-proof containers. If necessary, remove them from their wrappings and decant them into canisters or jars. Whole-grain products (wholemeal flour and pasta, brown rice, etc) cannot be kept as long as refined ones.

Dried herbs and spices will keep their flavour and scent best if stored in the dark. Light is their enemy, so store them in a cupboard or drawer, rather than on an open spice rack. Oil, too, should be stored in a cool dark place, in an airtight container. Refrigerate nut oils to preserve them longer.

Herbs and spices

The judicious use of a herb or spice, or both, can transform a dish. It's fun to experiment, once you know what you like and which seasonings go well with what foods.

Whenever possible, use fresh herbs, for their wonderful flavour, scent and colour. They're widely available in supermarkets and are also easy to grow, even in pots on a windowsill. Fresh herbs impart their flavour very quickly, so chop just before using and add to hot dishes towards the end of cooking. If fresh herbs are not available, you can, of course, substitute dried. Use them in a ratio of 1 teaspoon dried to 1 tablespoon fresh.

Most spices, both whole and ground, need time to impart their aroma and flavour to a dish. Some are pungent and spicy-hot, others are sweet and fragrant. If you can, grind spices freshly, using a spice mill, nutmeg grater or mortar and pestle. The difference in flavour and aroma between pre-ground and freshly ground is amazing.

GETTING THE TIMING RIGHT

Successful meal preparation is as much dependent on organization as on culinary skills. The initial planning of a menu – whether for the family supper or a dinner party – must give consideration to many things: a good range of flavours, colours and textures, as well as a balance in protein, fat, fibre and other healthy considerations.

That done, it then becomes a question of what you can prepare ahead, and what remains to be done at the last minute so that all is ready at the same time. For the beginner, this can be daunting.

The first step is to read all the recipes before making a final choice. The main dish, with simple accompaniments such as vegetables or a salad and bread, is a good starting point. Surround that with a cold starter (if there is to be one) and a cold dessert that can be made ahead of time. This way you can concentrate your efforts at each stage.

If you do choose two or more hot dishes, consider their cooking times and oven temperatures. If you have only one oven, and the temperatures required for the two dishes are different, this will present difficulties.

Next, make a shopping list. Check that you have all the equipment you require. Once you have everything to hand, you can start the preparation.

Read each recipe through again so you know what lies ahead, and try to estimate how long each preparation stage will take. Review techniques in the preparation that are unfamiliar, using the index to locate them, if necessary. Set the time you want to serve the meal, and work back from there so you know when to start the preparation. It's not a bad idea to write down all these times, as if you were planning military strategy.

If you are serving a starter, you'll need to plan what can be cooked unattended while you are at the table. If your chosen dessert is frozen, it may need some time out of the freezer before serving, so decide when to transfer it from freezer to refrigerator.

Remember to allow time for the final draining of vegetables, or carving of meat, or seasoning of a sauce. It is usually the case that all of these need to be done at the same time – but you only have one pair of hands. So decide what can wait and what will keep hot. Also allow time for plates to be cleared from the table if you are serving more than one course.

If any recipe requires the oven to be preheated or tins to be prepared, do this first. Pots of boiling salted water for cooking vegetables or pasta can be brought to the boil while you are doing the chopping and slicing.

Set out all the ingredients required and prepare them as specified in the recipe. If more than one dish calls for the same ingredients, say chopped onion or parsley, you can prepare the total amount at the same time.

Now start cooking, following your timetable. Check the recipe as you work, and don't be distracted. Keep tasting and sniffing the food as you go – that's much of the fun!

MEASURING TECHNIQUES

Cooks with years of experience may not need to measure ingredients, but if you are a beginner or are trying a new recipe for the first time, it is best to follow instructions carefully. Also, measuring ingredients precisely will ensure consistent results.

Both imperial and metric measures are given in this book. When preparing a recipe, use all imperial or all metric measures. Eggs are size 3 unless specified otherwise and recipes have been tested using a conventional not fan-assisted oven.

USEFUL CONVERSIONS

Imperial	Metric
1 teaspoon	a 5 ml spoon
3 teaspoons =	
1 tablespoon	a 15 ml spoon
¼ pint (5 fl oz)	150ml
½ pint (10 fl oz)	300ml
¾ pint (15 fl oz)	450ml
1 pint (20 fl oz)	600ml
1½ pints	900ml
2 pints	1.2 litres
1 oz	30 g
2 oz	55 g
3 oz	85 g
4 oz(¼ lb)	115 g
8 oz (½ lb)	225 g
12 oz (¾ lb)	340 g
1 lb (16 oz)	450 g
1 lb 2 oz	500 g
2¼ lb	1 kg
225°F/Gas ¼	110°C
250°F/Gas ½	130°C
275°F/Gas 1	140°C
300°F/Gas 2	150°C
325°F/Gas 3	170°C
350°F/Gas 4	180°C
375°F/Gas 5	190°C
400°F/Gas 6	200°C
425°F/Gas 7	220°C
450°F/Gas 8	230°C
475°F/Gas 9	240°C

1 ▲ **For liquids measured in fl oz or pints (ml or litres):** Use a glass or clear plastic measuring jug. Put it on a flat surface and pour in the liquid. Bend down and check that the liquid is level with the marking on the jug, as specified in the recipe.

2 ▲ **For liquids measured in spoons:** Pour the liquid into the measuring spoon, to the brim, and then pour it into the mixing bowl. Do not hold the spoon over the bowl when measuring because liquid may overflow.

3 ▲ **For measuring dry ingredients in a spoon:** Fill the spoon, scooping up the ingredient. Level the surface even with the rim of the spoon, using the straight edge of a knife.

4 ▲ **For measuring dry ingredients by weight:** Scoop or pour on to the scales, watching the dial or reading carefully. Balance scales give more accurate readings than spring scales.

5 ▲ **For measuring syrups:** Set the mixing bowl on the scales and turn the gauge to zero, or make a note of the weight. Pour in the required weight of syrup.

6 ▲ **For measuring butter:** Cut with a sharp knife and weigh, or cut off the specified amount following the markings on the wrapping paper.

POULTRY & MEAT

~

Poultry is always popular, and this chapter helps you make the
most of it. Clearly explained preparation and cooking
techniques show how simple it is to roast, stew and sauté meat,
as well as make great gravy and superb stock.

ROASTING POULTRY

Where would family gatherings be without the time-honoured roast bird? But beyond the favourite chicken, all types of poultry can be roasted – from small poussins to large turkeys. However, older tougher birds are better pot-roasted.

Protect and flavour
Before roasting, loosen the skin on the breast by gently easing it away from the flesh with your fingers. Press in softened butter – mixed with herbs or garlic for extra flavour – and smooth back the skin.

1 ▲ Wipe the bird inside and out with damp paper towels. Stuff the bird if the recipe directs and truss it. Spread the breast of chicken with softened or melted butter or oil; bard the breast of a lean game bird; prick the skin of duck and goose.

2 ▲ Set the bird breast up on a rack in a small roasting tin or shallow baking dish. If you are roasting a lean game bird, set the bird in the tin breast down.

3 ▲ Roast the bird, basting it every 10 minutes after the first ½ hour with the accumulated juices and fat in the tin. Turn if directed. If browning too quickly, cover loosely with foil.

4 ▲ Transfer the bird to a carving board and leave to rest for at least 15 minutes before serving. During that time, make a simple sauce or gravy with the juices in the tin.

Simple Roast Chicken
Squeeze the juice from a halved lemon over a 3–3½ lb (1.35–1.5 kg) chicken, then push the lemon halves into the body cavity. Smear ½ oz (15g) softened butter over the breast. Roast in a 375°F/190°C/Gas 5 oven for about 1¼ hours. Skim all fat from the roasting juices, then add 4 fl oz (120 ml) water and bring to the boil, stirring well to mix in the browned bits. Season with salt and pepper, and serve this sauce with the chicken. *Serves 4.*

ROASTING TIMES FOR POULTRY

Note: Cooking times given here are for unstuffed birds. For stuffed birds, add 20 minutes to the total roasting time.

Poussin	1–1½ lb (450–700 g)	1–1¼ hours at 350°F/180°C/Gas 4
Chicken	2½–3 lb (1.12–1.35 kg)	1–1¼ hours at 375°F/190°C/Gas 5
	3½–4 lb (1.5–1.8 kg)	1¼–1¾ hours at 375°F/190°C/Gas 5
	4½–5 lb (2–2.25 kg)	1½–2 hours at 375°F/190°C/Gas 5
	5–6 lb (2.25–2.7 kg)	1¾–2½ hours at 375°F/190°C/Gas 5
Capon	5–7 lb (2.25–3 kg)	1¾–2 hours at 325°F/170°C/Gas 3
Duck	3–5 lb (1.35–2.25 kg)	1¾–2¼ hours at 400°F/200°C/Gas 6
Goose	8–10 lb (3.6–4.5 kg)	2½–3 hours at 350°F/180°C/Gas 4
	10–12 lb (4.5–5.4 kg)	3–3½ hours at 350°F/180°C/Gas 4
Turkey (whole bird)	6–8 lb (2.7–3.6 kg)	3–3½ hours at 325°F/170°C/Gas 3
	8–12 lb (3.6–5.4 kg)	3–4 hours at 325°F/170°C/Gas 3
	12–16 lb (5.4–7.2 kg)	4–5 hours at 325°F/170°C/Gas 3
Turkey (whole breast)	4–6 lb (1.8–2.7 kg)	1½–2¼ hours at 325°F/170°C/Gas 3
	6–8 lb (2.7–3.6 kg)	2¼–3¼ hours at 325°F/170°C/Gas 3

Poussins Waldorf

SERVES 6

6 poussins, each weighing about 1¼ lb (575 g)

salt and pepper

1½–2 oz (45–55 g) butter, melted

FOR THE STUFFING

1 oz (30 g) butter

1 onion, finely chopped

10 oz (300 g) cooked rice

2 celery stalks, finely chopped

2 red apples, cored and finely diced

2 oz (55 g) walnuts, chopped

5 tablespoons cream sherry or apple juice

2 tablespoons lemon juice

1 Preheat a 350°F/180°C/Gas 4 oven.

2 For the stuffing, melt the butter in a small frying pan and fry the onion, stirring occasionally, until soft. Tip the onion and butter into a bowl and add the remaining stuffing ingredients. Season with salt and pepper and mix well.

3 ◀ Divide the stuffing among the poussins, stuffing the body cavities. Truss. Arrange in a roasting tin. Sprinkle with salt and pepper and drizzle over the melted butter.

4 Roast for about 1¼–1½ hours. Untruss before serving.

CARVING POULTRY

Carving a bird neatly for serving makes the presentation attractive. You will need a sharp long-bladed knife, or an electric knife, plus a long 2-pronged fork and a carving board with a well to catch the juices.

Cut away any trussing string. For a stuffed bird, spoon the stuffing from the cavity into a serving dish. For easier carving, remove the wishbone.

Insert the fork into one breast to hold the bird steady. Cut through the skin to the ball and socket joint on that side of the body, then slice through it to sever the leg from the body. Repeat on the other side.

1 ▲ Slice through the ball and socket joint in each leg to sever the thigh and drumstick. If carving turkey, slice the meat off the thigh and drumstick, parallel to the bone, turning to get even slices; leave chicken thighs and drumsticks whole.

2 ▲ To carve the breast of a turkey or chicken, cut ⅛–¼ in (3–5 mm) thick slices at an angle, slicing down on both sides of the breastbone. For smaller birds, remove the meat on each side of the breastbone in a single piece, then slice across.

Trussing Poultry

Trussing holds a bird together during cooking so that it keeps a neat, attractive shape. If the bird is stuffed, trussing prevents the stuffing falling out. You can truss with strong string or with poultry skewers.

An alternative to the method shown here is to use a long trussing needle and fine cotton string: make 2 passes, in alternate directions, through the body at the open end, from wing to wing, and tie. Then pass the needle through the parson's nose and tie the string around the ends of the drumsticks.

Remove all trussing before serving.

1 ▲ For an unstuffed bird: Set it breast down and pull the flap of neck skin over the neck opening. Turn the bird breast up and fold each wing tip back, over the neck skin, to secure firmly behind the shoulder.

2 ▲ Press the legs firmly down and into the breast. If there is a band of skin across the parson's nose, fold back the ends of the drumsticks and tuck them under the skin.

3 ▲ Otherwise, cross the knuckle ends of the drumsticks or bring them tightly together. Loop a length of string several times around the drumstick ends, then tie a knot and trim off excess string.

4 ▲ For a stuffed bird: Fold the wing tips back as above. After stuffing the neck end, fold the flap of skin over the opening and secure it with a skewer, then fold over the wing tips.

5 ▲ Put any stuffing or flavourings (herbs, lemon halves, apple quarters and so on) in the body cavity, then secure the ends of the drumsticks as above, tying in the parson's nose, too.

6 ▲ Alternatively, the cavity opening can be closed with skewers: insert 2 or more skewers across the opening, threading them through the skin several times.

7 ▲ Lace the skewers together with string. Tie the drumsticks together over the skewers.

Stuffing tips
When stuffing poultry, the stuffing should be cool, not hot or chilled. Pack it loosely into the bird because it will expand during cooking. Cook any left-over stuffing separately in a baking dish. Do not stuff poultry until just before putting it into the oven or pot. It is not a good idea to stuff the body cavity of a large bird because the stuffing could inhibit heat penetration, and thus not kill all harmful bacteria.

JOINTING POULTRY

Although chickens and other poultry are sold already jointed into halves, quarters, breasts, thighs and drumsticks, sometimes it makes sense to buy a whole bird and to do the job yourself. That way you can prepare 4 larger pieces or 8 smaller ones, depending on the recipe, and you can cut the pieces so the backbone and other bony bits (which can be saved for stock) are not included. In addition, a whole bird is cheaper to buy than pieces.

A sharp knife and sturdy kitchen scissors or poultry shears make the job of jointing poultry very easy.

Safe handling of raw poultry
Raw poultry may harbour potentially harmful organisms, such as salmonella bacteria, so it is vital to take care in its preparation. Always wash your hands, the chopping board, knife and poultry shears in hot soapy water before and after handling the poultry. It is a good idea to use a chopping board that can be washed at high temperature in a dishwasher and, if possible, to keep the chopping board just for the preparation of raw poultry. Thaw frozen poultry completely before cooking.

1 ▲ With the sharp knife, cut through the skin on one side of the body down to where the thigh joins the body. Bend the leg out away from the body and twist it to break the ball and socket joint.

2 ▲ Hold the leg out away from the body and cut through the ball and socket joint, taking the 'oyster meat' from the backbone with the leg. Repeat on the other side.

3 ▲ To separate the breast from the back, cut through the flap of skin just below the rib cage, cutting towards the neck. Pull the breast and back apart and cut through the joints that connect them on each side. Reserve the back for stock.

4 ▲ Turn the whole breast over, skin side down. Take one side of the breast in each hand and bend back firmly so the breastbone pops free. Loosen the bone on both sides with your fingers and, with the help of the knife, remove it.

5 ▲ Cut the breast lengthways in half, cutting through the wishbone. You now have 2 breasts with wings attached and 2 leg portions.

6 ▲ For 8 pieces, cut each breast in half at an angle so that some breast meat is included with a wing portion. Trim off any protruding bones.

7 ▲ With the knife, cut each leg portion through the ball and socket joint to separate the thigh and drumstick.

MAKING POULTRY SAUTÉS

A sauté combines frying and braising, producing particularly succulent results. It is a method suitable for pieces of poultry as well as for small whole birds such as quails and poussins.

As with frying, the poultry should be dried thoroughly with paper towels before cooking to ensure that it browns quickly and evenly.

1 ▲ Heat a little oil, a mixture of oil and butter, or clarified butter in a heavy frying pan or sauté pan.

2 ▲ Add the poultry and fry it over moderately high heat until it is golden brown, turning to colour evenly.

3 ▲ Add liquid and flavourings called for in the recipe. Bring to the boil, then cover and reduce the heat to moderately low. Continue cooking gently until the poultry is done, turning the pieces or birds over once or twice.

4 ▲ If the recipe instructs, remove the poultry from the pan and keep it warm while finishing the sauce. This can be as simple as boiling the cooking juices to reduce them or adding butter or cream for a richer result.

Country Chicken Sauté
Cook 6 oz (175 g) chopped bacon in 2 teaspoons oil over moderately high heat until lightly coloured. Remove and reserve. Dredge a 3½ lb (1.5 kg) chicken, cut into 8 pieces, in seasoned flour. Fry in the bacon fat until evenly browned. Add 3 tablespoons dry white wine and 8 fl oz (240 ml) poultry stock. Bring to the boil and add ½ lb (225 g) quartered mushrooms sautéed in 1 tablespoon of butter and the reserved bacon. Cover and cook over low heat for 20–25 minutes, or until the chicken is tender. *Serves 4.*

5 ▲ Thickening cooking juices:
Thicken with equal weights of butter and flour mashed together, called 'beurre manié'. Use 1 oz (30 g) of this paste to 8fl oz (240 ml) liquid. Whisk small pieces gradually into the boiling sauce until it is smooth and silky.

6 ▲ Another method of thickening cooking juices is to add a mixture of cornflour and water. Use 2 teaspoons cornflour blended with 1 tablespoon water to 8 fl oz (240 ml) liquid. Boil for 2–3 minutes, whisking constantly, until the sauce is syrup.

FRYING CHICKEN

Fried chicken is justifiably popular – crisp and brown outside and tender and juicy within. It's a quick and easy cooking method that can be applied to pieces of rabbit and hare and small turkey joints too.

Dry the pieces thoroughly with paper towels before frying. If they are at all wet, they will not brown properly. If the recipe directs, lightly coat the pieces with egg and crumbs or with a batter.

Succulent Fried Chicken
Mix 8 fl oz (240 ml) milk with 1 beaten egg in a shallow dish. On a sheet of greaseproof paper combine 5 oz (145 g) plain flour, 1 teaspoon paprika, and some salt and pepper. One at a time, dip 8 chicken pieces in the egg mixture and turn them to coat all over. Then dip in the seasoned flour and shake off any excess. Deep-fry for 25–30 minutes, turning the pieces so they brown and cook evenly. Drain on paper towels and serve very hot. *Serves 4*.

1 ▲ **For pan-frying:** Heat oil, a mixture of oil and butter, or clarified butter in a large, heavy-based frying pan over moderately high heat. When the oil is very hot, put in the chicken pieces, skin side down. Do not crowd them or they will not brown evenly; cook in batches if necessary.

3 ▲ **For deep-frying:** Dip the pieces into a mixture of milk and beaten egg, then coat lightly with seasoned flour; allow the coating to set for 20 minutes before frying. (Or coat them with a batter just before frying.)

5 ▲ With a fish slice or tongs, lower the chicken pieces into the oil, a few at a time, without crowding them. Deep-fry until they are golden brown all over and cooked. Turn them so they colour evenly.

2 ▲ Fry until deep golden brown all over, turning the pieces so they colour evenly. Fry until all the chicken pieces are thoroughly cooked. Remove pieces of breast before drumsticks and thighs (dark meat takes longer to cook than white meat). Drain on paper towels.

4 ▲ Half fill a deep pan with vegetable oil. Heat it to 365°F (185°C). You can test the temperature with a cube of bread: if it takes 50 seconds to brown, the oil is at the right temperature.

6 ▲ Drain on paper towels and serve hot. If you want to keep a batch of fried chicken hot while you fry the rest, put it into a low oven, but don't cover it or it will become soggy.

PREPARING MEAT FOR COOKING

You can buy meat ready for cooking from butchers and supermarkets. However, some cuts need further preparation, depending on how they are to be cooked. After stuffing, for example, a roast will need to be tied.

How much to buy

As a general guide, when buying boneless meat that has little or no fat, allow 5–7 oz (145–200 g) per serving. For meat with bone that has a little fat at the edge, allow about 8 oz (225 g) per serving. Very bony cuts such as shin and spareribs have proportionally little meat so you will need 1 lb (450 g) per serving.

1 ▲ **To trim:** Use a sharp knife to trim skin or rind and fat from the surface. Leave a little fat on steaks to be grilled, and slash this fat at regular intervals to prevent the steak curling up during cooking. Joints to be roasted should retain a thin layer of fat about ⅛–¼ in (3–5 mm). Cut away the sinews and tough connective tissue.

2 ▲ If you like, cut and scrape all fat and gristle from the ends of protruding bones (such as on cutlets or joints that contain rib bones). Cover the bone ends with foil to prevent charring.

3 ▲ **To chine a joint:** For large joints of meat that contain rib bones, such as rib of beef, pork loin and best end of lamb, it is a good idea to cut the chine bone (backbone) where it is joined to the rib bones, to loosen it or to remove it completely before cooking. Do this with a meat saw and sharp knife or ask your butcher to do it. Without the chine bone, the joint will be easy to carve.

4 ▲ **To bard a joint:** If a very lean piece of meat is to be roasted without a protective crust (a spice mixture, oil and crumbs or pastry, for example), it is a good idea to bard it to keep it moist. Wrap very thin slices of beef fat, pork fat or blanched bacon around the joint and tie them in place. Discard the fat before serving but keep the bacon, if liked.

5 ▲ **To tie a boned joint:** Joints that have been boned should be tied into a neat shape for roasting or pot roasting. The butcher will do this, but if you want to add a stuffing or seasoning, you will need to retie the joint yourself. Reshape it into a neat roll that is even in circumference. Use butcher's string to make ties around the circumference of the joint at 1 in (2.5 cm) intervals.

Boned Pork Loin with Apple Cream Sauce

SERVES 6

1 × 3 lb (1.35 kg) boned pork loin, rolled and tied

1 tablespoon fresh thyme leaves or 1 teaspoon dried thyme

salt and pepper

fresh thyme sprigs, watercress and sliced apples, to garnish

FOR THE SAUCE

⅔ oz (20 g) butter

1 onion, chopped

2 apples, such as Granny Smiths, peeled, cored and chopped

¼ pint (150 ml) whipping or double cream

1½ teaspoons Dijon mustard

1 tablespoon creamed horseradish

1 Preheat a 375°F/190°C/Gas 5 oven.

2 ▲ Untie the pork loin. Trim off the skin and most of the fat. Lay the pork out flat, skin side down. Sprinkle it with the thyme, salt and pepper and press into the meat.

~ COOK'S TIP ~

A boned joint will take longer to cook than the same weight joint with bone. This is because the bone conducts heat more readily than the flesh.

3 Roll up the loin again and tie it into a neat shape with string.

4 Put the pork loin on a rack in a small roasting tin. Roast for about 1 ¼–1 ½ hours or until well cooked.

5 ▼ Meanwhile, for the sauce, melt the butter in a saucepan and add the onion and apples. Cook over low heat for 20–25 minutes, stirring occasionally, until very soft.

6 ▲ Allow the apple mixture to cool slightly, then transfer it to a food processor. Add the cream, mustard and horseradish. Blend until smooth. Season with salt and pepper. Return the sauce to the pan and reheat just before serving.

7 When the pork is cooked, remove it from the oven to rest for about 10 minutes before carving. Garnish with thyme, watercress and apples.

ROASTING MEAT

The dry heat of oven roasting is best suited to tender cuts of meat. If they don't have a natural marbling of fat, bard them. Alternatively, marinate the meat or baste it frequently with the roasting juices during cooking.

Meat should be at room temperature for roasting. Roast on a rack in a tin that is just a little larger than the joint. Without a rack, the base of the joint would stew and not become crisp.

There are two methods of roasting meat. For the first, the joint is seared at a high temperature and then the heat is reduced for the remainder of the cooking time. For the second method, the joint is roasted at a constant temperature throughout. Scientific studies have shown that both methods produce good results, and that it is prolonged cooking, not the method, that affects juiciness and shrinkage. So use whichever method you prefer or follow the recipe.

Suggested roasting times
Following the second roasting method, in a 350°F/180°C/Gas 4 oven, approximate timings in minutes per 1 lb (450 g):
    Beef, rare, 20 + 20 extra*
        medium, 25 + 25 extra
        well done, 30 + 30 extra
    Veal, 25 + 25 extra
    Lamb, 25 + 25 extra
    Pork, 35 + 35 extra
(*Prime cuts such as rib of beef and tenderloin need less time.)

1 ▲ According to the recipe, rub the joint with oil or butter and season. If wished, for extra flavour, with the tip of a sharp knife make little slits in the meat all over the surface. Insert flavourings such as herbs, slivers of garlic, olive slices, shards of fresh ginger and so on.

2 ▲ Insert a meat thermometer in the thickest part, not touching a bone. (An instant-read thermometer is sometimes inserted towards the end of roasting.) Roast for the suggested time, basting if necessary.

3 ▲ Transfer the cooked meat to a carving board. Leave it to rest for 10–15 minutes before carving. During this time, make a gravy with the roasting juices, if liked.

Roast Leg of Lamb
Trim a 5–6 lb (2.25–2.7 kg) leg of lamb, removing almost all the fat. Cut 2–3 garlic cloves into very thin slices. Pull the leaves from 3 sprigs of fresh rosemary. Insert the garlic slices and rosemary leaves into slits in the lamb. Rub the lamb with olive oil and season with salt and pepper. Roast until cooked to your taste. *Serves* 8.

MEAT THERMOMETER READINGS

Beef		Lamb	
rare	125–130°F (52–54°C)	rare	130–135°F (54–57°C)
medium-rare	135°F (57°C)	medium	140–145°F (60–63°C)
medium	140–145°F (60–63°C)	well done	160°F (71°C)
well done	160°F (71°C)		
		Pork	
Veal		medium	150°F (66°C)
well done	160°F (71°C)	well done	160–165°F (71–74°C)

TESTING TO DETERMINE WHEN MEAT IS COOKED

The cooking times given in a recipe are intended to be a guideline. The shape of a cut can affect how long it takes to cook, and people have different preferences for how well cooked they like meat to be. So testing is essential.

Natural law of roasting

A joint will continue to cook in its own retained heat for 5–10 minutes after being removed from oven or pot, so it is a good idea to take it out when it is just below the desired thermometer reading.

---

1 ▲ Large joints that are roasted or pot-roasted can be tested with a metal skewer. Insert the skewer into the thickest part and leave it for 30 seconds. Withdraw the skewer and feel it: if it is warm, the meat is rare; if it is hot, the meat is well cooked.

2 ▲ The most reliable test is with the use of a meat thermometer, inserted in the centre of the joint, away from bones. Some instant-read thermometers are inserted at the end of cooking. Follow manufacturer's instructions. See the chart for the internal temperatures.

COOKING METHODS AND CHOICE OF CUTS

Roasting
Beef: rib (fore), wing or prime rib, middle rib, fillet, sirloin, topside, aitchbone
Veal: shoulder (oyster), best end of neck, loin, fillet, breast, leg, topside (cushion)
Lamb: shoulder, best end of neck (crown roast), saddle, loin, breast, leg (whole or divided into fillet and knuckle)
Pork: shoulder (spare rib), hand and spring, blade, loin, fillet (tenderloin), leg (whole or divided into fillet and knuckle), fresh belly, spareribs. Also gammon joints and bacon collar and hock

Pot-roasting and braising
Beef: brisket, silverside, top ribs, sirloin, topside, aitchbone, chuck, flank, rump (thick flank), braising steak
Veal: shoulder, best end of neck, middle neck cutlets, breast
Lamb: shoulder, middle neck cutlets, breast, loin, leg

Pork: shoulder (spare rib), loin, fillet (tenderloin). Also gammon joints and bacon collar and hock

Stewing
Beef: neck (clod or sticking), blade, chuck, shin, flank, leg, skirt
Veal: neck, shoulder, scrag, breast, knuckle (osso buco), stewing veal or pie veal
Lamb: middle neck, shoulder, breast, scrag end, chump chops
Pork: spare rib, fillet (tenderloin), loin

Pan-frying
Beef: fillet steak (tournedos), sirloin steak (porterhouse), rump steak, T-bone steak, entrecote, chateaubriand, hamburgers
Veal: cutlets, loin chops, chump chops, escalopes, fillet steaks
Lamb: cutlets, noisettes (boned cutlets), loin chops, chump chops, leg steaks, fillet
Pork: loin chops, spare rib chops, cubes or slices of fillet (tenderloin).

Also streaky and back bacon rashers, gammon rashers, gammon steaks, gammon chops

Grilling
Beef: fillet steak (tournedos), sirloin steak (porterhouse), rump steak, T-bone steak, hamburgers
Veal: cutlets, loin chops, chump chops, fillet steaks
Lamb: cutlets, noisettes (boned cutlets), loin chops, chump chops, leg steaks, cubes of fillet
Pork: loin chops, spare rib chops, cubes or slices of fillet (tenderloin). Also streaky and back bacon rashers, gammon rashers, gammon steaks, gammon chops

Stir-frying
Beef: strips or cubes of rump steak and other steaks
Veal: strips of escalope
Lamb: strips or cubes of shoulder fillet, leg
Pork: strips or cubes of fillet (tenderloin)

MAKING GRAVY

Gravy made from the roasting juices is rich in flavour and colour. It is a traditional accompaniment for roast meat and poultry.

For a thinner sauce, an alternative method to that explained here is deglazing, in which liquid is added to skimmed pan juices and then boiled to reduce it.

Resting a joint before carving
Once a joint is removed from the oven or pot, it should be left in a warm place to 'rest' for 10–15 minutes. During this time, the temperature of the joint evens out, and the flesh reabsorbs most of the juices. Thus, the juices won't leak during carving.

1 ▲ Spoon off most of the fat from the roasting tin. Set the tin over moderately high heat on top of the stove. When the roasting juices begin to sizzle, add flour and stir to combine well.

2 ▲ Cook, scraping the tin well to mix in all the browned bits from the bottom, until the mixture forms a smooth brown paste. Add stock or another liquid as specified in the recipe and bring to the boil, stirring or whisking constantly. Simmer until the gravy has the right consistency, then season with salt and pepper.

Rib of Beef with Shallots

SERVES 8

1 × 10 lb (4.5 kg) fore rib of beef (about 4 ribs), chined

vegetable oil

salt and pepper

1 lb (450 g) plump shallots, unpeeled

1½ tablespoons plain flour

12 fl oz (360 ml) beef stock or 8 fl oz (240 ml) beef stock and 4 fl oz (120 ml) red wine

1 Preheat a 350°F/180°C/Gas 4 oven.

2 If the ends of the rib bones have been left on the joint, scrape them clean, if wished. Rub any exposed bone ends with oil. Season the beef with salt and pepper. Set the joint in a roasting tin, fat side up.

3 Roast the beef until cooked to your taste, basting often with the juices in the tin.

4 ▲ Meanwhile, peel off the outer, papery layers of skin from the shallots, leaving at least 2 layers. Trim the root and stalk ends, if necessary.

5 About 30 minutes before the beef has finished cooking, put the shallots into the roasting tin round the beef.

6 When the beef is ready, transfer it to a carving board and set aside to rest for at least 15 minutes. Remove the shallots from the tin and keep warm.

7 ▼ Spoon off all but about 2 tablespoons of fat from the roasting tin. Make gravy in the tin with the roasting sediments, flour and stock.

8 Carve the rib of beef. Serve with the gravy, the shallots still in their skins (they slip out easily) and roast potatoes, if liked.

STEWING WITH A FRY START

Fry-start stews have a wonderful rich flavour, due greatly to the initial searing of the meat and vegetables. The long cooking period, in a seasoned liquid, produces a very tender result. Be sure to use a heavy-based pan or casserole.

Saving the flavour
If a different pan is used for searing the meat and vegetables, de-glaze it: add wine, stock or water and bring to the boil, scraping up the browned bits from the bottom of the pan. Then add the resulting liquid to the stewpot.

1 ▲ Cut the meat into equal-sized cubes and dry it thoroughly with paper towels. Coat lightly with flour if the recipe instructs.

2 ▲ Heat a little oil in a frying pan or flameproof casserole until it is very hot. Add a few cubes of meat – just enough to cover the bottom of the pan without touching each other. Do not crowd the meat in the pan. If the temperature drops too much, a crisp brown crust will not form.

3 ▲ Fry over moderately high heat until well browned on all sides. Turn the cubes so that they brown evenly, and remove them as they are done.

4 ▲ Add the vegetables and cook, stirring occasionally, until they are well browned. Discard excess oil if the recipe instructs.

5 ▲ Return the meat to the pan. If flour is added now, sprinkle it over the meat and vegetables and cook until it is well combined.

6 ▲ Add liquid barely to cover and stir to mix. Add any flavourings and bring the liquid to the boil. Reduce the heat to a gentle simmer and complete the cooking as specified.

7 ▲ If flour has not been used already, the liquid may be thickened at the end of cooking. One method is adding 'beurre manié', butter and flour paste, stirred in gradually.

8 ▲ Alternatively, thicken with cornflour mixed with water. Or remove the meat and vegetables and boil the liquid to reduce it and to concentrate the flavour.

Beef Stew with Dumplings

SERVES 4

1 oz (30 g) plain flour

salt and pepper

1½ lb (700 g) braising steak, cut into 1½ in (4 cm) cubes

3 tablespoons vegetable oil

2 large onions, chopped

2 celery stalks, coarsely chopped

2 large carrots, thickly sliced

2 turnips, cut into cubes

6 oz (170 g) swede, cut into cubes

¾ pint (450 ml) beef stock

1 tablespoon soy sauce

1 bay leaf

1½ teaspoons fresh thyme leaves or ½ teaspoon dried thyme

FOR THE DUMPLINGS

5 oz (145 g) flour

2 teaspoons baking powder

½ teaspoon salt

¼ teaspoon mustard powder

¼ pint (150 ml) milk

2 tablespoons vegetable oil

1 Combine the flour and some salt and pepper in a plastic bag. Add the beef cubes, a few at a time, and toss to coat them. Remove the cubes, shaking off excess flour.

2 ▲ Heat the oil in a flameproof casserole over moderately high heat. Add the cubes of beef, in batches, and brown them well on all sides. Remove them from the casserole as they are browned and set aside.

3 Add the onions, celery, carrots, turnips and swede. Brown them all over, stirring frequently.

4 ▲ Return the beef cubes to the casserole. Add the stock, soy sauce, bay leaf and thyme. Bring to the boil, stirring well to mix in the browned bits from the bottom of the pan.

5 Cover tightly, then reduce the heat to very low. Simmer for about 2 hours or until the beef is very tender.

6 For the dumplings, sift the dry ingredients into a bowl. Add the milk and oil and stir just until the dry ingredients are bound into a soft batter-like dough.

7 ▲ Uncover the casserole and bring the stew liquid back to the boil. Drop the dumpling dough on to the surface of the stew in 8–10 dollops.

8 Cover again and simmer over low heat for 12–15 minutes or until the dumplings are just set and fluffy. Serve immediately.

~ **VARIATION** ~

For Steak Pie, omit the dumplings and put the stew in a baking dish. Cover with puff pastry and bake at 400°F/200°C/Gas 6 for 25 minutes.

BROWNING OR SEARING MEAT

Large joints and pieces of meat to be roasted, pot-roasted or stewed are sometimes seared as the first step in their cooking. This may be done either by roasting briefly at a high temperature and then reducing the heat or by frying. The result is a browned crust that adds delicious flavour.

Pot-roasting

This method of cooking tenderizes even the toughest cuts of meat. Prime cuts can also be pot-roasted, but cooking times are cut short – just long enough to reach the degree of cooking you like.

Depending on the desired result, meat to be pot-roasted may or may not have an initial searing.

1 ▲ To sear by frying: Dry the meat well with paper towels. Heat a little oil in a frying pan, flameproof casserole or roasting tin until it is very hot. Put in the meat and fry over high heat until it is well browned on all surfaces. Turn the meat using two spatulas or spoons. (Piercing with a fork would let juices escape, which would be boiled away.)

2 ▲ If roasting, transfer the meat, in its roasting tin, to the oven. If pot-roasting, add a small amount of liquid and cover the pot tightly. If a frying pan has been used for searing, be sure to deglaze it: add some of the liquid called for in the recipe and bring to the boil, scraping up the browned bits from the bottom. Add this flavourful mixture to the pot.

Pot-roast Veal with Herbs

SERVES 6

1 tablespoon vegetable oil

1 × 3 lb (1.35 kg) boned veal shoulder, rolled and tied

4 medium onions, quartered

¼ pint (150 ml) chicken stock

a few sprigs each of fresh thyme, marjoram and rosemary or ¾ teaspoon each dried thyme, oregano and rosemary

salt and pepper

1 Preheat a 300°F/150°C/Gas 2 oven.

2 Heat the oil in a flameproof casserole over high heat (choose a casserole not much larger than the veal joint). Put in the veal joint and brown it, turning frequently to colour it evenly on all sides.

3 ▼ Add the onions, stock and herbs. Season with salt and pepper. Cover tightly and transfer to the oven. Cook for 2½–3 hours.

~ VARIATION ~

For Pot-roast Pork with Herbs, substitute a boned pork shoulder or hand and spring.

4 ▲ Remove the veal joint and onions and set aside on a carving board. Leave the veal to rest for at least 10 minutes before carving, discarding the strings.

5 Skim the cooking juices to remove all fat. Bring to the boil, then strain. Taste for seasoning. Serve with the veal and onions.

PAN-FRYING AND SAUTÉING

Tender cuts of meat, such as steaks and chops, slices of calf's liver and hamburgers, are ideal for cooking quickly in a heavy frying pan. And the juices left in the pan can be turned into an easy sauce.

Before pan-frying and sautéing, trim excess fat from steaks, chops, escalopes, etc, then dry them very thoroughly with paper towels.

For cooking, use a fat that can be heated to a high temperature. If using butter, an equal amount of vegetable oil will help prevent burning, or use clarified butter.

1 ▲ Heat the fat in the pan over high heat until very hot but not browning. Put in the meat, in one layer. Do not crowd the pan.

2 ▲ Fry until browned on both sides and done to your taste. If pan-frying pork or veal chops, reduce the heat to moderate once they are in the pan.

Testing steak
A reliable way to test steak is by pressing it with your finger. When raw, it is soft and can be squashed. When cooked rare, it will be only slightly springy. When cooked medium, it will offer more resistance and drops of red juice will appear on the surface. When well done, it will be firm to the touch.

Pan-fried Teriyaki Steak
Combine 3 tablespoons vegetable oil, 1 tablespoon each soy sauce, honey, red wine vinegar and finely chopped onion, 1 crushed garlic clove and ½ teaspoon ground ginger in a plastic bag. Add 4 rump or sirloin steaks and turn to coat well. Put the bag in a dish and marinate for 2 hours. Drain the steaks and pat dry, then pan-fry until cooked to your taste. The steaks can also be grilled. *Serves 4.*

DEGLAZING FOR A PAN SAUCE

After pan-frying or sautéing, a simple yet delicious sauce can be made in the pan. The same method can be used to make gravy for roast meats. It is also a good way to maximize flavour in stews and casseroles.

Before deglazing, remove the meat and keep it warm. Pour or spoon off all the fat from the pan, unless the recipe calls for shallots, garlic, or the like to be softened. In that case, leave 1–2 teaspoons of fat and cook the vegetables in it.

1 ▲ Pour in the liquid called for in the recipe (wine, stock, vinegar, etc). Bring to the boil, stirring well to scrape up all the browned bits from the bottom of the pan and dissolve them in the liquid.

2 ▲ Boil over high heat for 1–2 minutes or until the liquid is almost syrupy. If the recipe instructs, enrich the sauce with cream or butter. Season to taste with salt and pepper and serve.

STIR-FRYING

The preparation of ingredients for stir-frying often takes longer than the cooking itself. This is because all ingredients must be cut to uniform sizes so that the cooking can be accomplished quickly and evenly.

A wok is excellent for stir-frying because its high sides let you stir and toss the ingredients briskly. Use long cooking chopsticks or a wooden spatula to keep the ingredients moving around the wok.

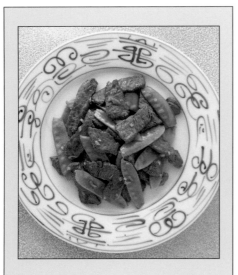

Stir-fried Beef with Mange-tout
Cut 1 lb (450 g) lean boneless tender beef into very thin strips. Combine 3 tablespoons soy sauce, 2 tablespoons dry sherry, 1 table-spoon brown sugar and ½ tea-spoon cornflour in a bowl. Heat 1 tablespoon vegetable oil in the hot wok. Add 1 tablespoon each finely chopped fresh ginger and garlic and stir-fry for 30 seconds. Add the beef and stir-fry for 2 minutes or until well browned. Add 8 oz (225 g) mange-tout; stir-fry for 3 minutes. Stir the soy sauce mixture until smooth, then add to the wok. Bring to the boil, stirring and tossing, and simmer just until it is thickened and smooth. Serve immediately, accompanied by freshly boiled rice. *Serves 4.*

1 ▲ Prepare all the ingredients in uniformly sized pieces following recipe instructions.

2 ▲ Heat a wok or large deep frying pan over moderately high heat. Dribble in the oil down the sides.

3 ▲ When the oil is hot (a piece of vegetable should sizzle on contact), add the ingredients in the order specified in the recipe. (Those that take longer to cook are added first.) Do not add too much to the wok at a time or the ingredients will start to steam rather than fry.

4 ▲ Fry, stirring and tossing constantly with chopsticks or a spatula, until the ingredients are just cooked: vegetables should be crisp-tender and meat and poultry tender and juicy.

5 ◀ Push the ingredients to the side of the wok or remove them. Pour liquid or sauce as specified in the recipe into the bottom. Cook and stir, then mix in the ingredients from the side. Serve immediately.

MAKING MEAT STOCK

The most delicious meat soups, stews, casseroles, gravies and sauces rely on a good home-made stock for success. Neither a stock cube nor a canned consommé will do if you want the best flavour. Once made, meat stock can be kept in the refrigerator for 4–5 days, or frozen for longer storage (up to 6 months).

On the light side
For a light meat stock, use veal bones and do not roast the bones or vegetables. Put in the pot with cold water and cook as described.

MAKES ABOUT 3½ PINTS (2 LITRES)

4 lb (1.8 kg) beef bones, such as shin, leg, neck and clod, or veal or lamb bones, cut into 2½ in (6 cm) pieces
2 onions, unpeeled, quartered
2 carrots, roughly chopped
2 celery stalks, with leaves if possible, roughly chopped
2 tomatoes, coarsely chopped
7½ pints (4.5 litres) cold water
a handful of parsley stalks
a few fresh thyme sprigs or ¾ teaspoon dried thyme
2 bay leaves
10 black peppercorns, lightly crushed

1 ▲ Preheat a 450°F/230°C/Gas 8 oven. Put the bones in a roasting tin or flameproof casserole and roast, turning occasionally, for 30 minutes or until they start to brown.

2 ▲ Add the onions, carrots, celery and tomatoes and baste with the fat in the tin. Roast for a further 20–30 minutes or until the bones are well browned. Stir and baste occasionally.

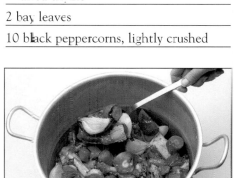

3 ▲ Transfer the bones and vegetables to a stockpot. Spoon off the fat from the roasting tin.

4 ▲ Add a little of the water to the roasting tin or casserole and bring to the boil on top of the stove, stirring well to scrape up any browned bits. Pour this liquid into the stockpot.

5 ▲ Add the remaining water. Bring just to the boil, skimming frequently to remove all the foam from the surface. Add the parsley, thyme, bay leaves and peppercorns.

6 ▲ Partly cover the pot and simmer the stock for 4–6 hours. The bones and vegetables should always be covered with liquid, so top up with a little boiling water from time to time if necessary.

7 ▲ Strain the stock through a sieve. Skim as much fat as possible from the surface. If possible, cool the stock and then refrigerate it; the fat will rise to the top and set in a layer that can be removed easily.

FISH & SEAFOOD

~

*Fish and seafood are simple to cook and excellent for a quick
meal. The techniques show ways to cook fish by baking,
grilling, poaching and frying methods, how to make fish stock,
and how to prepare live shellfish.*

PREPARING WHOLE FISH FOR COOKING

Most fish have scales and these should be removed before cooking unless the fish is to be filleted or the skin is to be removed before serving. Fish sold by fishmongers will normally be scaled as well as cleaned (eviscerated or gutted), but you can do this yourself, if necessary. Trimming the tail gives a whole fish a neat appearance.

   All fish preparation is best done in or near the sink, with cool water running. Salt your hands for a good grip on the fish.

1 ▲ **To scale:** Grasp the tail firmly and scrape off the scales using a special fish scaler or a knife, working from the tail towards the head. Rinse the fish well. Repeat on the other side.

2 ▲ **To trim:** For flat fish to be cooked whole, use kitchen scissors to trim off the outer half of the small fin bones all round the fish.

3 ▲ For round fish, cut the flesh on both sides of the anal and dorsal (back) fins and pull them out; the small bones attached will come out too. Trim off the other fins.

4 ▲ If the fish is to be cooked whole, leave the fins on, or just trim them, because they help keep the shape of the fish.

5 ▲ **To trim the tail:** If the tail is to be left on, cut a neat 'V' in the centre with scissors. The fish is now ready for cooking.

A LOOK AT FISH

In terms of shape and structure, most fish fall into one of two general categories: round fish and flat fish.

   Round fish have thicker bodies and many of their bones are attached to their fins. They can be filleted or cut into steaks or cutlets, but all will contain small pin bones.

   Flat fish have a flat central bone with a row of bones attached on either side. This simple bone structure makes flat fish easy to fillet. Most are too thin to cut into steaks or cutlets.

   Large fish such as tuna have a thick bone running down the centre of their bodies; spiking out from this are four rows of bones that divide the flesh into quarters. These boneless 'loins' are usually sliced into steaks.

   The fat content of fish is an important consideration in deciding how to cook it. Lean fish can dry out at high temperatures, so a protective coating is a good idea when frying. When grilling, marinate or baste them. Lean and moderately lean fish are best cooked by moist methods such as steaming, poaching and baking in sauce. Oily fish, however, almost baste themselves during cooking, so

they are ideal for baking, grilling and pan-frying.

   Texture and flavour are also important in choosing how to prepare fish. If the flavour of the flesh is mild, it is important not to overwhelm it. But fish with rich, distinctively flavoured flesh will stand up well to spicy, pungent seasonings.

   Fish that are delicate in texture need careful cooking. Pan-frying with a flour coating, steaming and gentle baking are best. However, fish with meaty, dense flesh can be cubed and put on to skewers.

Pan-fried Trout with Olives and Capers

SERVES 4

4 whole trout, ¾–1 lb (340–450 g) each, gutted and trimmed

salt and pepper

flour, for coating

4 tablespoons vegetable oil

3 oz (85 g) butter

3 oz (85 g) black olives, sliced

3 tablespoons capers

2 tablespoons lemon juice

lemon wedges, to serve

1 ▲ Sprinkle the trout with salt and pepper. Coat them lightly with flour, shaking off any excess.

Terms used by fishmongers
Cutlet: Thickish slice cut cross-ways from the middle of a whole gutted fish.
Escalope: Thin slice cut on a slant from a large fillet.
Fillet: Boneless or nearly boneless piece cut lengthways from the sides of the fish. May or may not be skinned.
Gutted: Describes fish that has had its internal organs removed. Other terms used are cleaned and eviscerated.
Steak: Thickish slice cut cross-ways from the tail end of a whole gutted fish.

2 ▲ Heat the oil in a large frying pan over moderate heat. Add the trout and fry for 12–15 minutes or until golden on both sides and cooked.

3 Transfer the trout to a warmed serving platter and keep warm. Pour off all the oil from the pan.

4 ▼ Add the butter to the frying pan and melt it. When it starts to brown and smell nutty, stir in the olives, capers and lemon juice. Cook for 10 seconds, then pour this sauce over the fish. Serve immediately.

BAKING FISH

Most fish are suitable for baking – whole or in fillets, cutlets or steaks. Lean fish, in particular, benefit from some protection to prevent them from drying out: choose recipes that include a stuffing or coating or bake them in a little liquid or sauce, which can also be served with the fish. All of these add extra flavour to the fish too.

Cooking in foil or paper parcels is suitable for many fish, both small whole ones and pieces (fillets, cutlets or steaks). This seals in moisture, so the effect is similar to steaming.

A good rule of thumb to calculate cooking time for fish is 10 minutes in a 425°F/220°C/Gas 7 oven for each 1 in (2.5 cm), measured at the thickest part.

1 ▲ To bake fish with liquid, pour over a small amount of stock, wine, water or other liquid as specified in the recipe, then add seasonings.

2 ▲ To bake fish in foil or paper, wrap, tightly with seasonings and flavourings as specified and place the parcel on a baking sheet.

Baked Fish Steaks
Arrange 1½ lb (700 g) white fish steaks in a shallow baking dish. Sprinkle the fish with 2 table-spoons chopped shallot or onion and 3 tablespoons lemon juice or dry white wine. Drizzle with 1 oz (30 g) melted butter and season with salt and pepper. Bake in a 425°F/220°C/Gas 7 oven for ab-out 10 minutes or until the fish is cooked. Pour the cooking juices over the steaks before serving.
Serves 4.

A SELECTION OF FISH VARIETIES

Choose the freshest fish you can find. If necessary, substitute another variety with similar qualities.

Lean fish
Bream
- round fish, saltwater
- firm, moist texture; delicate, sweet flavour
- fry, grill, bake, steam
- substitute red mullet, John Dory

Brill
- flat fish, saltwater
- fine texture, delicate flavour
- fry, grill, bake, steam, poach
- substitute other flat fish, such as turbot, John Dory

Cod
- round fish, saltwater
- flaky, tender texture; mild flavour
- grill, bake, steam, poach
- substitute haddock, halibut

Haddock
- round fish, saltwater
- soft, moist texture; mild flavour
- grill, bake, steam, poach
- substitute cod, halibut

Hake
- round fish, saltwater
- white flesh with good flavour
- grill, bake, steam, poach
- substitute cod, haddock

Halibut
- flat fish, saltwater
- firm, moist texture; mild, sweet flavour
- grill, bake, steam, poach
- substitute plaice, sole

John Dory
- flat fish, saltwater
- flaky texture; nutty sweet flavour
- poach, bake, grill, steam
- substitute brill, halibut

Plaice
- flat fish, saltwater
- fine texture; delicate flavour
- fry, grill, bake, steam
- substitute sole, other flat fish

Sea bass
- round fish, saltwater
- flaky or firm flesh; mild flavour
- grill, fry, bake
- substitute salmon, grey mullet, John Dory

TESTING TO DETERMINE WHEN FISH IS COOKED

All seafood cooks quickly. If overcooked it becomes dry and loses its succulent quality. In the case of meaty fish such as tuna and swordfish, it can be unpleasantly chewy. It is therefore worth knowing how to judge when fish is perfectly cooked.

The flesh of raw fish and crustaceans is translucent; it becomes opaque when it is cooked.

1 ▲ To determine whether a fish is cooked, make a small slit in the thickest part. Lift with the knife to look into the opening.

2 ▲ The fish is ready when still very slightly translucent in the centre or near the bone (it will continue to cook when removed from the heat).

Skate
- flattened body with large fins (wings), saltwater
- flaky, well-flavoured flesh
- fry, grill, poach, steam

Sole (Dover and lemon)
- flat fish, saltwater
- fine texture; delicate flavour
- fry, grill, bake, poach
- substitute plaice

Turbot
- flat fish, saltwater
- succulent; firm yet tender; superb flavour
- bake, grill, poach, steam
- substitute brill, John Dory

Moderately lean fish
Grey mullet
- round fish, saltwater
- delicate, easily digested flesh
- fry, grill, poach, bake

Monkfish
- round, saltwater
- firm texture; sweet, similar to lobster
- fry, grill, bake, poach, stew
- substitute cod, halibut

Red mullet
- round fish, saltwater
- delicate texture with excellent flavour
- grill, bake, fry
- substitute trout

Swordfish
- thick central bone, saltwater
- firm, meaty texture; mild but distinctive flavour
- grill, bake, steam, poach
- substitute dogfish/rock salmon, tuna

Trout
- round fish, freshwater
- tender, flaky texture; delicate, rich
- fry, grill, bake
- substitute sea trout, small salmon

Tuna
- thick central bone, saltwater
- some varieties more oily
- firm, meaty texture; mild to strong flavour
- bake, steam, poach, grill
- substitute swordfish, dogfish/rock salmon

Moderately oily and oily fish
Carp
- round fish, freshwater
- soft, flaky texture; mild flavour
- bake, grill, fry, steam
- substitute cod, haddock

Herring
- round fish, saltwater
- moist and tender; rich flavour
- grill, bake, fry, souse
- substitute mackerel

Mackerel
- round fish, saltwater
- moist and tender or firm texture; rich, distinctive flavour
- grill, bake, fry, souse
- substitute herring

Salmon
- round fish, freshwater/saltwater
- flaky, tender texture; mild to rich
- bake, grill, steam, poach
- substitute large sea trout

Sea trout/salmon trout
- round fish, saltwater
- moist, flaky texture; mild, sweet
- grill, bake, fry
- substitute salmon, rainbow trout

POACHING FISH

Whole fish, large and small, as well as fillets, cutlets and steaks are excellent poached because the gentle cooking gives succulent results. Poached fish can be served hot or cold, with a wide variety of sauces. The poaching liquid may be used as the basis for the sauce.

Poaching containers

A long rectangular fish kettle with a perforated rack enables you to lift the fish out of the liquid after cooking. You could also use a large wire rack set in a deep tin.

1 ▲ To oven-poach small whole fish, fillets, cutlets or steaks: Place the fish in a buttered flameproof dish that is large enough to hold the pieces comfortably. Pour in enough liquid to come two-thirds of the way up the side of the fish.

2 ▲ Add any flavourings called for in the recipe. Press a piece of buttered greaseproof on top to keep in the moisture without sticking to the fish.

3 ▲ Set the dish over moderate heat and bring the liquid just to the boil. Transfer the dish to a 350°F/180°C/ Gas 4 oven and poach until the fish is just cooked. To test, with the tip of a sharp knife, make a small cut into the thickest part of the fish (ideally near a bone): the flesh should be slightly translucent.

4 ▲ To poach whole fish, fillets, cutlets or steaks on top of the stove: Put large whole fish on the rack in a fish kettle, or set on a piece of muslin that can be used like a hammock. Small whole fish, fillets, cutlets and steaks may be poached in a fish kettle on a rack, or set directly in a wide saucepan or frying pan.

5 ▲ Prepare the poaching liquid (salted water, milk, wine, stock or court bouillon) in the fish kettle or in a large casserole or roasting tin (or a wide saucepan or frying pan for fillets, cutlets and steaks). Set the rack in the kettle, or the muslin hammock in the casserole or tin. Add more liquid, if necessary, to cover the fish.

6 ▲ Cover the kettle or casserole and bring the liquid just to the boil. Reduce the heat and simmer very gently until the fish is cooked.

Poached Sole Fillets

Oven-poach 8 skinless sole fillets, about 1½ lb (700 g), each ½ in (1.5 cm) thick. Use ½ pint (300ml) dry white wine or fish stock with 4–6 chopped spring onions, 4–6 lemon slices and a few allspice berries for flavouring. Simmer for 3–5 minutes, then remove the fish. Boil the cooking liquid until reduced to 4 tablespoons, then strain it. Season with salt and pepper. *Serves 4.*

STEAMING FISH

This simple, moist-heat method of cooking is ideal for fish and shellfish. If you don't have a steamer, it is easy to improvise.

Steamed Salmon with Herbs
Line a heatproof plate with fresh herb sprigs (dill, parsley, chives etc). Set 2 portions of seasoned salmon fillet, each 1 in (2.5 cm) thick, on top. Steam Chinese-style for about 10 minutes. If you like, top with a flavoured butter or serve with Hollandaise sauce. *Serves 2.*

1 ▲ Using a steamer: Arrange the fish on the rack in the steamer and set over boiling water. Cover and steam until done.

2 ▲ Chinese-style steaming: Arrange the fish on a heatproof plate that will fit inside a bamboo steamer or wok. Put the plate on the rack in a steamer or wok; set over boiling water. Cover and steam until done.

3 ▲ Steaming larger fish and fillets: Arrange the fish on a rack in a roasting tin of boiling water or on a plate set on the rack. Cover tightly with foil and steam until done.

4 ▲ Steaming in foil: Wrap the fish and seasonings in foil, sealing well, and set on a rack in the steamer or in a large roasting tin of boiling water. Steam until done.

CUTTING FISH STEAKS AND CUTLETS

Round fish and large flat fish such as halibut are often cut into steaks and cutlets for cooking. Steaks are cut from the tail end of the fish, while cutlets are cut from the centre. They are usually cut about 1–1½ in (2.5–4 cm) thick.

1 ▲ With a large, sharp knife, slice the fish across, at a right angle to the backbone, into slices of the desired thickness.

2 ▲ If necessary, cut through the backbone with kitchen scissors or a knife with a serrated blade.

CUTTING FISH FILLETS

Fillets are boneless pieces of fish, and for this reason are very popular. A sharp filleting knife, with its thin, flexible blade, is the tool to use for removing the fillets. Be sure to keep all the bones and trimmings for making stock.

Round fish are easy to fillet and they produce a boneless piece from each side. Large flat fish are also easy to deal with, although they are filleted slightly differently from round fish and they yield 4 narrow fillets – 2 from each side.

Filleting small flat fish
You can take 2 fillets from smaller flat fish (one from each side): Cut behind the head and down the sides of the fish as above, but do not make the central cut. Starting from the head end on one side and working down the fish, cut the flesh away from the rib bones until you reach the centre (the backbone). Rotate the fish and repeat on the other side to cut away the whole fillet. Turn the fish over and repeat to cut away the second whole fillet.

1 ▲ To fillet a round fish: Lay the fish flat, on its side. First cut off the head. With the tip of the knife, cut through the skin all along the length of the backbone.

3 ▲ When you reach the tail, cut across to release the fillet. Repeat the procedure on the other side to remove the other fillet.

2 ▲ Working from head to tail and holding the knife almost parallel to the fish, use short strokes to cut 1 fillet off the rib bones in one piece. Follow the slit cut along the backbone.

4 ▲ Run your fingers over the flesh side of each fillet to locate any stray bones. Pull them out with tweezers.

5 ▲ To fillet a flat fish: Lay the fish flat and make a curved cut behind the head, cutting down to but not through the backbone. With the tip of the knife, slit the skin down both sides of the fish where the fin bones meet the rib bones, 'outlining' the fillets, and slit across the tail.

6 ▲ Slit straight down the centre line of the fish, from head to tail, cutting down to the backbone. Working from the centre at the head end, cut 1 fillet neatly away from the rib bones on one side. Hold the knife blade almost parallel to the fish and use short strokes.

7 ▲ Rotate the fish and cut away the second fillet. Turn the fish over and repeat to remove the 2 fillets on the other side. Pull out any stray bones with tweezers.

GRILLING FISH

The intense dry heat of this method of cooking is best used for fish with a lot of natural oil, such as salmon, mackerel and tuna. However, leaner fish can also be grilled, as long as you baste them frequently to keep them moist or cook them in a little liquid.

Always preheat the grill. If liked, line the grill pan with foil to save on washing up.

Fish can also be very successfully grilled over charcoal. Choose full-flavoured fish that will not be overwhelmed by the smoky taste. Thin pieces are easier to handle if placed in a hinged wire fish basket. Be sure to baste well during cooking to prevent the fish from drying out.

Fish Kebabs with Lemon Butter
Combine 2 tablespoons each melted butter and lemon juice with 1 teaspoon mustard powder and 1 finely chopped garlic clove. Cut 1 ½ lb (700 g) halibut, monkfish or sea bass steaks into 1 in (2.5 cm) cubes. Thread on to skewers with pieces of red pepper. Brush with the butter mixture and grill, basting frequently and turning to cook evenly, until done. *Serves 4.*

1 ▲ To grill oilier fish: For small whole fish, boned and butterflied fish, fillets, cutlets and steaks that are at least ½ in (1.5 cm) thick, or cubes of fish for skewers, rinse the fish and pat it dry with paper towels. Marinate the fish if the recipe instructs.

3 ▲ Set the fish under the grill, 3–4 in (7.5–10 cm) from the heat (thin pieces should be closer to the heat for a shorter time than thicker ones). Grill, basting once or twice and turning if the recipe specifies, until the fish is done.

2 ▲ Preheat the grill with the grill pan in place. When hot, lightly brush the hot pan with oil. If using foil, line it before preheating and then brush with oil when hot. Arrange the fish in the pan, in one layer, skin side down. Brush the fish with butter, oil or a basting mixture, according to the recipe instructions.

4 ▲ To grill leaner fish: For small whole fish, and fish steaks, cutlets and fillets that are at least ½ in (1.5 cm) thick and prepared for cooking as above, arrange in a buttered flameproof dish. Add a little liquid (wine, stock etc) just to cover the bottom of the dish. Brush the fish with butter, oil or a basting mixture, according to recipe instructions. Grill as above, without turning the fish.

COATING AND FRYING FISH

Fish to be fried is often coated with egg and crumbs, or with a batter. The coating makes a crisp crust to protect the fish and keep it moist. Many other foods – boneless chicken breasts, veal escalopes and vegetables, for example – are also egg-and-crumbed.

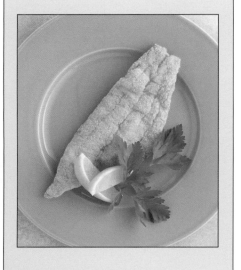

Deep-fried Catfish
Egg-and-crumb 8 catfish (or trout) fillets, using seasoned flour, egg and cornmeal. Deep-fry and serve with tartare sauce. *Serves 4*.

1 ▲ Lightly beat egg in a shallow dish. Spread flour on a plate or sheet of greaseproof paper and season with salt and pepper or as specified. Spread crumbs (fine breadcrumbs, crushed water biscuits, etc) on another.

2 ▲ **To egg-and-crumb large pieces of fish:** Dip the fish first in the seasoned flour, turning to coat both sides lightly and evenly. Shake or brush off excess flour.

3 ▲ Next dip the floured fish in the egg, turning to moisten both sides.

4 ▲ Dip the fish in the crumbs, turning to coat evenly. Press to help the crumbs adhere. Shake or pat off excess crumbs. Refrigerate for at least 20 minutes to set the coating.

5 ▲ **To egg-and-crumb small pieces of fish** (strips of fish fillet or goujons, prawns, etc): Put the crumbs in a plastic bag. After dipping the fish in seasoned flour and egg, toss a few pieces at a time in the bag of crumbs.

6 ▲ **To pan-fry:** Heat oil or a mixture of oil and butter in a frying pan (enough fat to coat the bottom of the pan in a thin layer or as recipe instructs). When it is very hot, put the fish in the pan, in one layer. Fry until golden brown on both sides and the fish is done. Drain on paper towels before serving.

7 ▲ **To deep-fry:** Half fill a deep pan with oil and heat it to 375°F (190°C) on a deep-frying thermometer. Gently lower the coated pieces of fish into the hot oil (frying them only a few at a time). Fry until golden brown, turning them occasionally so that they cook evenly. Remove and drain on paper towels before serving.

PREPARING MUSSELS AND CLAMS

Molluscs such as mussels and clams should be eaten very fresh and must be alive when you buy them and cook them (unless they have been shelled and frozen). You can tell that they are alive if their shells are tightly closed; any shells that are open should close promptly when tapped. Any dead mussels or clams, or any with broken shells, should be discarded.

If you have collected clams yourself, let them stand in a bucket of sea water for several hours, changing the water once or twice. (Do not use fresh water because it will kill the molluscs.) Add a handful or two of cornmeal or flour to the water to help clean the clams' stomachs. Clams bought from the fishmonger will already have been purged of sand.

Sailor's Mussels
Prepare 7 pints (4 litres) live mussels. Steam with ½ pint (300 ml) dry white wine or fish or chicken stock, 1 small chopped onion, 1–2 crushed garlic cloves and ¾ oz (25 g) chopped fresh parsley. With a slotted spoon, transfer the opened mussels to large bowls. Add 1½ oz (45 g) butter to the cooking liquid and stir until melted, then add pepper. Pour over the mussels. *Serves 4.*

1 ▲ Scrub the shells of mussels or clams with a stiff brush and rinse well. This can be done under cool running water.

3 ▲ To steam: Put a little dry white wine or water in a large pot, with flavourings as the recipe specifies. Add the mussels or clams, cover tightly and bring to the boil. Steam for 5–10 minutes or until the shells open, shaking the pot occasionally.

5 ▲ To open a live clam or mussel: Hold it firmly in one hand, with the hinge in your palm. Insert the side of a clam or oyster knife blade between the shell halves and work it round to cut through the hinge muscle.

2 ▲ Before cooking mussels, pull off their 'beards' (their anchor threads) with the help of a small knife. Rinse the mussels well.

4 ▲ Serve the mussels or clams in their shells, or shell them before using. Strain the cooking liquid (which will include all the delicious liquor from the shells) and spoon it over the mussels or clams, or use it as the basis for a sauce.

6 ▲ Open the shell and cut the clam or mussel free of the shell. Do this over a bowl to catch all the liquor from the shell. (Clams may be eaten raw, but mussels are always cooked.)

PEELING AND DEVEINING PRAWNS

Prawns can be cooked in their shells, but more often they are peeled first (the shells can be used to make an aromatic stock). The intestinal vein that runs down the back is removed from large prawns mainly because of its appearance, although the vein may contain grit which makes it unpleasant to eat.

Prawns in shell are sold with their heads. These are easily pulled off, and will enhance the flavour of stock made with the shells.

1 ▲ Holding the prawn firmly in one hand, pull off the legs with the fingers of the other hand. Pull off the head above the legs.

2 ▲ Peel the shell away from the body. When you reach the tail, hold the body and pull away the tail; the shell will come off with it. Or, you can leave the tail on the prawn and just remove the body shell.

3 ▲ Make a shallow cut down the centre of the curved back of the prawn. Pull out the black vein with a cocktail stick or your fingers.

4 ▲ To butterfly prawns: Cut along the deveining slit to split open the prawn, without cutting all the way through. Open up the prawn flat.

5 ▲ To devein prawns in the shell: Insert a cocktail stick crossways in several places along the back where the shell overlaps to lift out the vein.

Spicy Butterflied Tiger Prawns

SERVES 4–6

6 tablespoons olive oil

5 tablespoons orange juice

4 tablespoons lime juice

1 large garlic clove, finely chopped

1 teaspoon allspice berries, crushed

¼ teaspoon hot chilli flakes

salt and pepper

2 lb (900 g) raw tiger or king prawns, peeled, deveined and butterflied

lime wedges, to serve

1 ▲ Combine the oil, fruit juices, garlic, allspice, chilli flakes and seasoning in a large shallow baking dish. Add the prawns and turn to coat completely with the spiced oil.

2 Cover the dish and leave to marinate for 1 hour at room temperature or at least 2 hours in the refrigerator.

3 Preheat the grill.

4 Spread out the prawns in one layer in the baking dish, arranging them cut side up as much as possible. Grill about 4 in (10 cm) from the heat for 6–8 minutes or until the flesh becomes opaque. There is no need to turn them.

5 Serve hot, with lime wedges.

Scallops Wrapped in Parma Ham

SERVES 4

24 medium-size scallops, without corals,
  prepared for cooking

lemon juice

8–12 slices of Parma ham, cut
  lengthways into 2 or 3 strips

olive oil

pepper

lemon wedges, to serve

1 Preheat the grill or prepare a charcoal fire.

2 Sprinkle the scallops with lemon juice. Wrap a strip of Parma ham around each scallop. Thread on to 8 skewers.

3 ▲ Brush with oil. Arrange on a baking sheet if grilling. Grill about 4 in (10 cm) from the heat, or cook over charcoal, for 3–5 minutes on each side or until the scallops are opaque.

4 Set 2 skewers on each plate. Sprinkle the scallops with freshly ground black pepper and serve with lemon wedges.

Preparing scallops

If they are still in the shell, use a short sturdy knife to pry open scallops, as for clams. Discard the fringe-like membrane and dark organs. Set the red-orange coral, or roe, aside.

  Pull off and discard the small piece of gristle from the side of the white meat. Rinse well.

Spicy Butterflied Tiger Prawns (left), Scallops Wrapped in Parma Ham

MAKING FISH STOCK

Fish stock is much quicker to make than meat or poultry stock. Ask your fishmonger for heads, bones and trimmings from white fish.

MAKES ABOUT 2 PINTS (1 LITRE)

1½ lb (700 g) heads, bones and trimmings from white fish
1 onion, sliced
2 celery stalks with leaves, chopped
1 carrot, sliced
½ lemon, sliced (optional)
1 bay leaf
a few fresh parsley sprigs
6 black peppercorns
2¼ pints (1.35 litres) water
¼ pint (150 ml) dry white wine

1 ▲ Rinse the fish heads, bones and trimmings well under cold running water. Put in a stockpot with the vegetables, lemon, if using, the herbs, peppercorns, water and wine. Bring to the boil, skimming the surface frequently, then reduce the heat and simmer for 25 minutes.

2 ▲ Strain the stock without pressing down on the ingredients in the sieve. If not using immediately, leave to cool and then refrigerate. Fish stock should be used within 2 days, or it can be frozen for up to 3 months.

Fisherman's Stew

SERVES 4

6 streaky bacon rashers, cut into strips
½ oz (15 g) butter
1 large onion, chopped
1 garlic clove, finely chopped
2 tablespoons chopped fresh parsley
1 teaspoon fresh thyme leaves or ½ teaspoon dried thyme
1 lb (450 g) tomatoes, skinned, seeded and chopped or canned chopped tomatoes
¼ pint (150 ml) dry vermouth or white wine
¾ pint (450 ml) fish stock
10 oz (300 g) potatoes, diced
1½–2 lb (700–900 g) skinless white fish fillets, cut into large chunks
salt and pepper

1 Fry the bacon in a large saucepan over moderate heat until lightly browned but not crisp, then remove the bacon and drain on paper towels.

2 ▲ Add the butter to the pan and cook the onion, stirring occasionally, for 3–5 minutes or until soft. Add the garlic and herbs and continue cooking for 1 minute, stirring. Add the tomatoes, vermouth or wine and stock and bring to the boil.

3 Reduce the heat, cover and simmer the stew for 15 minutes. Add the potatoes, cover again and simmer for a further 10–12 minutes or until they are almost tender.

4 ▼ Add the chunks of fish and the bacon. Simmer gently, uncovered, for 5 minutes or until the fish is just cooked and the potatoes are tender. Adjust the seasoning and serve.

~ COOK'S TIP ~

For fish stock, use heads, bones and trimmings only from mild, white-fleshed fish, not from strong-flavoured oily fish.

PASTA, GRAINS & PULSES

~

*These staple foods are nutritious and simple to cook, offering
a delicious alternative to meat. This chapter looks at ways
of preparation and cooking techniques, and shows you how
to make your own pasta.*

COOKING PASTA

Both fresh and dried pasta are cooked in the same way. The golden rules for success are: use plenty of water and keep checking the pasta to be sure it does not overcook.

Fresh pasta will cook much more quickly than dried – in 1–4 minutes as opposed to 5 minutes or more.

1 ▲ Bring a very large pot of salted water to the boil: use at least 6 pints (4 litres) of water and 2 teaspoons salt to 1 lb (450 g) of pasta. Drop in the pasta all at once and stir to separate the shapes or strands.

2 ▲ If you are cooking spaghetti, allow the ends in the water to soften slightly and then gently push in the rest as soon as you can.

Buttered Noodles
Cook 1 lb (450 g) fettuccine or tagliatelle (fresh or dried) until 'al dente'. Drain well and return to the pot. Add 1 ½–2 oz (45–55 g) butter or margarine and a good pinch of grated nutmeg. Season. Toss until the noodles are coated, then serve. *Serves 6.*

Buttered Noodles with Herbs
Omit the nutmeg and add ½ oz (15 g) chopped fresh herbs such as parsley, dill, basil or thyme – singly or a mixture.

Buttered Noodles with Cheese
Add 3 tablespoons freshly grated Parmesan cheese.

3 ▲ Bring the water back to the boil, then reduce the heat slightly and boil until the pasta is just done. For dried pasta, follow the packet instructions, but start testing as soon as you reach the minimum time given. To test, lift a piece of pasta out on a wooden fork or slotted spoon. Cut it in half. There should be no sign of opaque, uncooked pasta in the centre. Or bite it – it should be tender but still firm. In Italian, this is when it is 'al dente', or to the tooth.

4 ▲ Drain the pasta well in a colander, shaking it vigorously to remove all excess water. Serve immediately because the pasta will continue to cook from its own heat.

When to undercook pasta
If you are going to cook the pasta further, by baking it in a lasagne for example, undercook it slightly at this first stage. Pasta for a salad should also be a little under-cooked, so that it will not be-come soggy when it is mixed with the dressing.

MAKING PASTA DOUGH

Pasta dough is very simple to make and, like most things, the more you do it the better the results will be. As in making pastry and bread doughs, the quantity of liquid needed can vary, according to how absorbent the flour is. The recipe here is for a basic egg pasta, with several variations.

MAKES ABOUT 1 LB (450 G)

10 oz (300 g) plain flour, preferably 'type 00' pasta flour

1 teaspoon salt

3 size-2 eggs, beaten to mix

1 ▲ Put the flour and salt on a work surface and make a well in the centre. Add the eggs to the well.

2 ▲ With fingertips, gradually incorporate the flour into the eggs. When all the flour is mixed in, you should be able to gather up a pliable dough; if too moist, add more flour.

Pasta flavourings

● For *Green Pasta:* Blanch 12 oz (340 g) spinach, Swiss chard or other green leaves, then drain well and squeeze dry. Purée or chop the greens very finely. Add with the eggs.

● For *Fresh Herb Pasta:* Finely chop 1 oz (30 g) fresh herb leaves, such as basil, flat-leaf parsley and coriander. Add with the eggs.

● For *Tomato Pasta:* Add 1½ tablespoons tomato purée with the eggs.

● For *Lemon Pasta:* Add 1½ tablespoons grated lemon zest with the eggs.

● For *Herb and Garlic Pasta:* Add ½ oz (15 g) finely chopped mixed parsley and oregano or marjoram and 1–2 finely chopped garlic cloves with the beaten eggs.

● For *Saffron Pasta:* Add ½ tea-spoon ground saffron to the flour and salt or steep ½ teaspoon saf-fron threads in 1 tablespoon very hot water and add with the eggs through a small sieve.

● For *Wholemeal Pasta:* Substi-tute 2½ oz (75 g) wholemeal flour for the same quantity of plain flour.

3 ▲ Flour the work surface. Knead the dough by pushing it away with the heel of your hand and then folding it back. Continue kneading for about 8–10 minutes or until it is smooth and elastic. (Alternatively, use a pasta machine for kneading.)

4 ▲ Shape the dough into a ball and put it in a bowl. Cover with cling film. Leave to rest for at least 15 minutes before rolling and cutting.

Food processor pasta dough

To mix the pasta dough in a food processor, put the flour and salt in the container. Pulse to blend. With the machine running, gradu-ally add the eggs through the feed tube. Continue processing for 3–5 minutes or until the ingredients come together into a smooth ball of dough that is elastic.

ROLLING AND CUTTING PASTA DOUGH BY HAND

You can roll pasta dough by hand, but it is hard work. If you intend to make pasta frequently, it may be worth buying a machine.

Divide the dough into 3 or 4 pieces. Roll and cut one piece at a time. Keep the remaining dough tightly wrapped in cling film to prevent it from drying out while you work.

Pasta with Ham and Peas
Cook 2 finely chopped garlic cloves in 1 oz (30 g) of butter in a saucepan for 1 minute or until softened. Add 5 oz (145 g) thawed frozen peas, 8 oz (225 g) cooked ham cut into matchstick strips, ½ pint (300 ml) whipping cream and seasoning and bring to the boil. Toss with 12 oz (340 g) fresh fettuccine, cooked and drained, and 2 oz (55 g) freshly grated Parmesan cheese. Serve at once, with additional Parmesan cheese if wished. *Serves 4.*

Keeping fresh pasta
If fresh noodles are not to be cooked the day they are made, allow them to dry completely. Then wrap loosely and store at room temperature for up to 4 days.

1 ▲ Put a piece of dough on a lightly floured surface and pat it into a flat disc. Using a long rolling pin, roll out the dough in all directions, starting from the centre each time.

3 ▲ For stuffed pasta shapes, use the dough immediately, while it is still malleable. If cutting noodles, sprinkle the rolled out dough with flour and leave to dry for 10–15 minutes.

5 ▲ Uncoil the noodles with your fingers and scatter them on a floured tea towel. Leave to dry for about 5 minutes before cooking. Alternatively, wrap in cling film and refrigerate for later cooking.

2 ▲ Continue rolling, with long even strokes, until you have a large sheet of dough that is about ⅛ in (3 mm) thick, or less for thinner noodles.

4 ▲ To cut, roll up the sheet of dough like a flat Swiss roll. With a knife, cut across into noodles of the required width: ⅛ in (3 mm) for fettuccine, ¼ in (5 mm) for tagliatelle.

6 ▲ To dry, leave them on the floured towel, or hang them over a broom handle, and dry for 2–3 hours. Sprinkle them with semolina to prevent them sticking together and pack loosely in a plastic bag or in a box with each layer separated.

USING A PASTA MACHINE

A pasta machine – hand-cranked or electric – takes all the drudgery out of making fresh pasta. You are able to roll the dough paper-thin and to cut very fine noodles such as tagliolini and tagliarini – impossible by hand.

The smooth rollers on a pasta machine can be set wide apart or very close together, normally with the use of a dial. You start at the widest setting to knead the dough and then reduce the space gradually until the dough reaches the right thickness. Then a roller with blades cuts noodles of the desired width.

1 ▲ To knead dough: Flatten a piece of the dough slightly and then feed it through the machine's rollers on their widest setting.

2 ▲ Fold the resulting strip of dough in half and feed it through again. Continue folding the dough and feeding it through until smooth and elastic, 8–10 times. (If it feels sticky, dust it with flour before continuing.)

Lemon Pasta with Clam Sauce
Cook 2–3 finely chopped garlic cloves in 5 tablespoons olive oil for 1 minute or until softened. Add 8 oz (225 g) steamed shelled clams, chopped if large, with 3 tablespoons of their cooking liquid, or canned baby clams (*vongole*), drained. Heat the clams through, then add 4 tablespoons chopped parsley and 2–3 tablespoons lemon juice. Toss the sauce with 12 oz (340 g) fresh lemon pasta, cooked and drained, and freshly ground pepper. Serve immediately. *Serves 4.*

3 ▲ To roll dough: Adjust the rollers to the next narrower setting and feed the strip of dough through again, without folding it. Narrow the rollers again and feed the strip of dough through. Continue feeding the dough through the rollers at increasingly narrow settings until it is the desired thinness. Sprinkle with flour and dry for 10–15 minutes.

4 ▲ To cut noodles: Set the blades on the machine to the desired width. Feed the strip of dough through the blades, letting it fall on to a floured tea towel. Dry for about 5 minutes before cooking. (Or dry completely for longer storage.)

Drying out
It is important to leave the pasta dough to dry before cutting it into noodles, or they will tend to stick together. If the day is humid, this initial drying can take up to 30 minutes.

CUTTING FLAT PASTA SHAPES

For wide noodles, like pappardelle, and for pasta for layering or rolling up, such as lasagne and cannelloni, roll the dough by hand or machine to about ⅛ in (3 mm) thickness. Lay the rolled dough strip, which will be about 4–5 in (10–12.5 cm) wide, on a lightly floured surface. Trim the sides to make them straight and square, using a sharp knife or, for pappardelle, a fluted pasta wheel. Lasagne may also be cut with a wheel for a decorative fluted edge.

1 ▲ To make lasagne or cannelloni: For lasagne, cut the dough strip into rectangles about 10–12 in (25–30 cm) long, or to fit your baking dish. For cannelloni, cut into rectangles about 5 × 3 in (12.5 × 7.5 cm).

2 ▲ For pappardelle: Cut the strip of dough into long noodles about ⅝ in (1.5 cm) wide. These noodles are traditionally cut with a fluted pasta wheel, and need not be uniform as they are meant to be rustic.

Tuna Lasagne

SERVES 6

1 quantity fresh pasta dough, cut for lasagne, or 12 oz (340 g) oven-ready dried lasagne
½ oz (15 g) butter
1 small onion, finely chopped
1 garlic clove, finely chopped
4 oz (115 g) mushrooms, thinly sliced
4 tablespoons dry white wine (optional)
1 pint (600 ml) white sauce
¼ pint (150 ml) whipping cream
3 tablespoons chopped parsley
salt and pepper
2 × 7 oz (200 g) cans tuna, drained
2 canned pimientos, cut into strips
2½ oz (75 g) thawed frozen peas
4 oz (115 g) mozzarella, grated
1 oz (30 g) freshly grated Parmesan cheese

1 For fresh lasagne noodles, bring a large pot of salted water to the boil. Cook the noodles, in small batches, until almost tender to the bite. For dried noodles, soak in a bowl of hot water for 3–5 minutes.

2 ▲ Lift out noodles into a colander and rinse with cold water. Lay them on a tea towel, in one layer, to drain.

3 Preheat a 350°F/180°C/Gas 4 oven.

4 ▲ Melt the butter in a saucepan. Cook the onion until soft. Add the garlic and mushrooms. Cook until they are soft, stirring occasionally.

5 Pour in the wine, if using. Boil for 1 minute. Add the white sauce, cream and parsley. Season to taste.

6 Spoon a thin layer of sauce over the bottom of a 12 × 9 in (30 × 23 cm) baking dish. Cover with a layer of lasagne noodles. Flake the tuna. Strew half of the tuna, pimiento strips, peas and mozzarella over the noodles. Spoon one-third of the remaining sauce evenly over the top and cover with another layer of lasagne noodles.

7 ▲ Repeat the layers, ending with noodles and sauce. Sprinkle with the Parmesan. Bake for 30–40 minutes or until bubbling hot and the top is lightly browned. Cut into squares and serve from the baking dish.

COOKING RICE

There are many different ways to cook rice, and each has its adherents. The simplest is to cook rice in a large quantity of boiling water, then drain. However, valuable nutrients will be discarded in the water. The ways given here retain the rice's nutrients. Timings are for long-grain white rice (one part rice to two parts water).

Rice Salad
Steam or bake 6 oz (170g) long-grain rice. While hot, dress with 6 tablespoons vinaigrette. Cool. Add 2 oz (55 g) each chopped spring onions, celery, radishes, cucumber and quartered black olives with another 4 fl oz (120 ml) vinaigrette. Combine well and sprinkle with chopped parsley. *Serves 4–6.*

2 ▲ **To sauté and steam rice (pilaf):** Heat oil, butter or a mixture of the two in a saucepan over moderate heat. Add the rice and stir to coat the grains. Sauté for 2–3 minutes, stirring constantly. Add the measured quantity of boiling salted water. Bring back to the boil, then cover and steam over very low heat until the water has been absorbed and the rice is tender.

1 ◀ **To steam rice:** Put the measured quantity of salted water in a saucepan and bring to the boil. Add the rice and stir. Bring back to the boil, then cover the pan and steam over very low heat until the rice has absorbed all the water and is tender, 15–18 minutes for white rice and 35–40 minutes for brown rice. Remove the pan from the heat and leave for 5 minutes, covered. To serve, fluff the rice with a fork.

3 ▲ **To bake rice:** Put the rice in a baking dish and add the measured quantity of boiling salted water. Cover tightly with foil or a lid and bake in a preheated 350°F/180°C/Gas 4 oven until the water has been absorbed and the rice is tender, 20–30 minutes for white rice and 35–45 for brown. Cooking time depends on many factors, including the seal of the dish.

A LOOK AT RICE

There are thousands of varieties of rice grown all over the world, with differing flavours and aromas. But for the cook, the choice of which rice to use in a dish is based mainly on the length of the rice grain.

Long-grain rice has grains that are four to five times as long as they are wide. It is dry and fluffy after cooking, with the grains remaining separate. Examples of long-grain rice include: Basmati (aromatic, with a rich nutty flavour; much used in Indian cooking), brown long-grain rice (husk removed but nutritious bran layer left; texture is slightly chewy, mild nutty flavour), and white or polished long-grain rice (most widely used; mild in flavour). Long-grain rice is excellent steamed or baked, in pilafs and salads.

Short-grain rice, with an almost round shape, is very starchy and tends to cling together after cooking. Examples of short-grain rice include: Arborio and Carnaroli rice (used in creamy textured dishes) and glutinous or sweet rice (very sticky after cooking; used in Oriental desserts and snacks). Short-grain rice is the one to use for puddings, risotto, croquettes, sushi, stir-fried rice and moulded rice dishes.

Medium-grain rice, in between the other two, is more tender than long-grain rice but less moist than short-grain. It is fluffy and separate if served hot, but clumps as it cools.

COOKING WILD RICE

Although called 'rice', this is actually an aquatic grass. Its deliciously nutty flavour and firm chewy texture make it a perfect complement to many meat and poultry dishes. It is also an excellent partner for vegetables such as courgettes, patty pan squash and mushrooms. It can be cooked like rice, by boiling or steaming, needing only a longer cooking time.

1 ▲ **To boil wild rice:** Add the rice to a large pot of boiling salted water (about four parts water to each one of rice). Bring back to a gentle boil and cook for 45–50 minutes or until the rice is tender but still firm and has begun to split open. Drain well.

2 ▲ **To steam wild rice:** Put the rice in a saucepan with the measured quantity of salted water. Bring to the boil, cover and steam over very low heat for 45–50 minutes or until tender. Cook uncovered for the last 5 minutes to evaporate excess water.

Wild Rice and Turkey Salad

SERVES 4

6 oz (170 g) wild rice, boiled or steamed

2 celery stalks, thinly sliced

2 oz (55 g) spring onions, chopped

4 oz (115 g) small button mushrooms, quartered

1 lb (450 g) cooked turkey breast, diced

4 fl oz (120 ml) vinaigrette dressing, made with walnut oil

1 teaspoon fresh thyme leaves

2 pears, peeled, halved and cored

1 oz (30 g) walnut pieces, toasted

1 ▲ Combine cooled cooked wild rice with the celery, spring onions, mushrooms and turkey in a bowl.

2 ◄ Add the dressing and thyme and toss well together.

3 Thinly slice the pear halves lengthways without cutting through the stalk end and spread the slices like a fan. Divide the salad among 4 plates. Garnish each with a fanned pear half and walnuts.

PREPARING PULSES

Pulses – dried beans, peas and lentils – are a high-protein food. They keep well, making them a useful storecupboard staple. Most pulses require the same initial preparation.

An extra safeguard
To remove potentially harmful toxins, boil most pulses uncovered for 10 minutes before reducing the heat to a simmer for the rest of the cooking time.

1 ▲ First rinse the pulses and pick out any small stones.

2 ▲ **To soak dried beans and peas:** Put them in a bowl, cover with plenty of cold water and soak for at least 4 hours. (Lentils do not need soaking.)

3 ▲ A quick alternative method is to put the dried beans or peas in a large pan of water, bring to the boil and boil for 2 minutes, then leave them to soak for 1 hour.

4 ▲ In either case, drain the pulses and rinse them well. They are now ready for cooking according to the recipe.

5 ▲ **To cook:** Put the soaked and drained beans or peas or the lentils in a pan of fresh cold water (3 parts water to 1 part pulses) and bring to the boil. Then cover the pan, reduce the heat and simmer until tender.

A LOOK AT PULSES

Dried beans, peas and lentils range widely in colour, shape and size. Some of the most commonly available include: **haricot beans,** large to medium-sized, kidney-shaped, white; **kidney beans,** medium-sized, kiney-shaped, smooth, shiny, may be reddish-brown, black or white (when normally called cannellini beans); **flageolet,** small, oval, pale green; **black beans** (also called turtle beans), small, oval, smooth, shiny, jet-black; **borlotti beans,** medium-sized, kidney-shaped, creamy brown with red streaks; **pinto beans,** small, oval,

smooth, beige with brown specks; **black-eye beans,** small, oval, smooth, creamy colour, with small cream-centred black dot on one side; **butter beans,** large, oval/round, flattish, off-white; **chickpeas,** medium-sized, round, not smooth, beige-tan in colour; **peas,** small, round or split in half, may be grey-green or yellow; **lentils,** tiny, disc-shaped, smooth, may be brownish-green, reddish-orange or yellow.

Pulses are easy to prepare, and they can be used in many ways – in casseroles, soups, stews and salads.

The minimum soaking time for most dried pulses is 4 hours, but they can be soaked overnight if that is more convenient. Lentils do not need soaking, and it is not essential for split peas, although they may be soaked to speed cooking.

Most pulses require about 1½–2 hours' cooking time. This includes white haricot beans, borlotti beans, pinto beans, butter beans, kidney beans and chickpeas. Black-eye beans, split peas and flageolet beans require less time, about 1–1¼ hours. Lentils cook in less than 30 minutes.

PREPARING BULGAR WHEAT

Bulgar wheat, a nutritious grain, is made by steaming whole wheat berries and then drying and cracking them into very small pieces. Cook like rice, either steamed plain or as a pilaf, or soak it to rehydrate. Serve as an accompaniment or use in salads.

Cooking simple bulgar pilaf
Soften 1 small finely chopped onion in 1 oz (30 g) butter. Add 6 oz (170 g) bulgar wheat, ¾ pint (450 ml) chicken stock and a bay leaf. Cover and steam. Season and add 2 tablespoons chopped parsley.

1 ▲ **To steam bulgar:** Use two parts liquid to one part bulgar. Put the bulgar in a saucepan with water or other liquid such as stock, add flavourings if directed and bring to the boil. Cover and simmer over low heat for 12–15 minutes or until tender.

2 ▲ **To soak bulgar:** Put the bulgar in a sieve and rinse under cold running water until the water runs clear. Put the bulgar in a bowl, cover with fresh cold water and soak for 1 hour or until plump. Drain, pressing out all excess moisture.

Bulgar Wheat Salad with Herbs

SERVES 6

4 oz (115 g) bulgar wheat, soaked and well drained

8 oz (225 g) tomatoes, seeded and diced

1 small red onion, chopped

3 spring onions, chopped

2 oz (55 g) parsley, finely chopped

4 tablespoons chopped fresh mint

4 fl oz (120 ml) olive or vegetable oil

5 tablespoons lemon juice

salt and pepper

black olives and mint leaves, to garnish

1 ▲ Combine all the ingredients in a large bowl.

2 ◄ Stir to mix the ingredients thoroughly. Taste and adjust the seasoning if necessary.

3 Serve the salad at room temperature, garnished with black olives and mint leaves, if liked.

VEGETABLES

~

*Using the wide variety of fresh vegetables available today, this
vegetable primer shows preparation techniques and the
different cooking methods suitable for each one. There are
creative recipes, serving ideas and a method for making stock.*

PREPARING AND COOKING VEGETABLES

To enjoy their full flavour, fresh vegetables are often best prepared and served simply. These guidelines for vegetable preparation and cooking will help you make the most of seasonal bounty.

Serving ideas include suggested amounts of raw prepared vegetable to serve per person. Season all dishes to taste. Recipes in these sections serve 4.

ROOTS AND BULBS
Carrots
Naturally sweet, carrots are used in innumerable dishes, and are tasty hot and cold, raw and cooked.

Preparation: If they are young, there is no need to peel them; just trim the ends and scrub well. Larger carrots should be peeled. Leave whole or cut as specified. If carrots have a woody core, cut it out.

Cooking: *To boil*, drop into boiling salted water and simmer until just tender: 8–10 minutes for whole baby carrots, 10–20 minutes for larger whole carrots, 4–10 minutes for sliced or grated carrots. *To steam*, cook whole baby carrots, covered, over boiling water for about 10 minutes. *To braise*, cook whole baby carrots or thinly sliced carrots, with

3 tablespoons stock or water and 1 oz (30 g) butter per 1 lb (450 g), tightly covered, for about 5 minutes. Boil, uncovered, to evaporate excess liquid before serving.

Serving ideas (4 oz/115 g each)
● Dress hot carrots with butter and chopped fresh herbs such as parsley, chives, thyme or marjoram.
● Add a little sugar or honey and a squeeze of lemon or orange juice when braising. Or, try spices such as nutmeg, ginger or curry powder.
● Serve raw carrot sticks with a dip.

Parsnips
Their sweet, nutty flavour makes a delicious addition to soups and stews or enjoy them on their own.

Preparation: Trim the ends and peel thinly. Leave small parsnips whole; cut up larger ones. If large parsnips have a woody core, cut it out.

Cooking: *To roast*, blanch in boiling salted water, then put in a roasting tin with butter or oil and cook in a 400°F/200°C/Gas 6 oven for about 40 minutes. Baste occasionally. *To boil*, drop into boiling salted water and simmer for 5–10 minutes or until just tender. *To fry*, blanch in boiling water

for 1–2 minutes and drain. Fry in butter for 10–12 minutes or until golden brown and tender.

Serving ideas (5 oz/145 g each)
● Mix 1 ¼ lb (600 g) boiled parsnips, 2 oz (55 g) butter and 4 tablespoons honey; cook, covered, for 5 minutes.
● Sauté sliced parsnips with sliced carrots; sprinkle with chopped herbs.
● Bake 1¼ lb (600 g) small parsnips with ¼ pint (150 ml) orange juice and 1½ oz (45 g) butter, covered, in a 350°F/180°C/Gas 4 oven for 1 hour.
● Roast blanched parsnips in the tin around a joint of beef or pork.

Turnips
Mildly piquant, turnips go well with both sweet and savoury seasonings.

Preparation: Trim the ends and peel the turnips thinly.

Cooking: *To steam*, cook cubes, covered, over boiling water for about 15 minutes or until tender. *To boil*, drop into boiling salted water and simmer until tender: 20–30 minutes if whole, about 7 minutes if diced. *To braise*, cook thin slices, with 1 oz (30 g) butter and 5 tablespoons stock or water, in a covered pan, for 4–5 minutes.

Serving ideas (4 oz/115 g each)

● Mash boiled turnips with milk and butter; mix with an equal quantity of mashed carrots, parsnips or potatoes.

● Cover 1 lb (450 g) steamed turnips with 1 pint (600 ml) hot white sauce, sprinkle with breadcrumbs and grated cheese; brown under the grill.

● Add 1 tablespoon sugar when braising turnips; uncover and boil to evaporate excess liquid and to caramelize the turnips.

Swede

The orangey-yellow flesh of this root vegetable is sweet and full of flavour.

Preparation: Peel, removing all tough skin and roots. Cut as recipe specifies.

Cooking: *To boil*, put chunks into boiling salted water and simmer for 15 minutes or until tender. Do not overcook or the vegetable will be watery and mushy. *To steam*, cook slices, covered, over boiling water for 9–12 minutes or until tender. *To braise*, cook, with 1 oz (30 g) butter and 5 tablespoons stock or water per 1 lb (450 g), covered, for 5–7 minutes. *To roast*, put chunks or sticks around roasting meat and turn to coat with the dripping. Roast at 400°F/200°C/Gas 6 for about 45 minutes.

Serving ideas (5 oz/145 g each)

● Braise 1¼ lb (600 g) grated swede seasoned with 1 tablespoon soft brown sugar and 1 teaspoon soy sauce.

● Mash 1¼ lb (600 g) boiled swede until smooth; beat in 2 eggs, 4 tablespoons cream, 2 tablespoons flour and ¼ teaspoon nutmeg until fluffy. Bake in a buttered dish in a 350°F/180°C/Gas 4 oven for about 30 minutes.

Potatoes

Boiling potatoes are moist with a waxy texture so they keep their shape when cooked. Baking potatoes are dry and starchy and their texture is more floury after cooking. In addition, there are orange- and white-fleshed sweet potatoes.

Preparation: If the potato skins will be eaten, scrub them well. Otherwise, peel potatoes.

Cooking: *To bake*, prick skins all over with a fork and bake in a 400°F/200°C/Gas 5 oven until tender: 1–1½ hours or 30–40 minutes for sweet potatoes. *To boil*, put into a pan of cold salted water, bring to the boil, and simmer until just tender: 10–20 minutes according to size. *To roast*, blanch peeled potatoes for 1–2 minutes; drain and pat dry. Put

around meat in a roasting tin and turn to coat with dripping; roast for 1–1½ hours, turning occasionally. *To sauté*, boil until partly cooked (in skin if specified), then fry slices or cubes in butter or oil until brown and crisp.

To deep-fry (chips), cut into sticks and soak in cold water for at least 30 minutes; drain and pat dry. Fry (in small batches) in oil heated to 375°F/190°C until beginning to colour: 3–7 minutes according to size. Drain on paper towels, then fry again for 3 minutes or until golden brown and crisp.

Stuffed Jacket-baked Potatoes

Cut baked potatoes in half and scoop out the centres, leaving a thin wall of flesh. Mash the scooped-out flesh with a little butter and 3 tablespoons each grated Cheddar cheese and diced cooked ham per potato. Season to taste. Fill the potato shells with the mixture, mounding it. Sprinkle the tops with grated Cheddar, then bake at 400°F/200°C/Gas 6 for 10–15 minutes.

Serving ideas (6 oz/170 g each)

- Dress boiled new potatoes with butter and chopped mixed parsley and mint or toasted pine nuts.
- Mash boiled or baked sweet potatoes with an electric mixer. Add butter to taste, orange juice to moisten and ground cinnamon. Season and beat well.

Celeriac

The coarse knobby appearance of celeriac belies its delicate and delicious flavour.

Preparation: Peel off the thick skin. Do this just before cooking because celeriac discolours when cut. If serving it raw, drop the peeled root or pieces into water acidulated with lemon juice or vinegar. Cut as instructed in recipe.

Cooking: *To steam*, cook cubes, covered, over boiling water until tender. *To boil*, drop cubes into boiling salted water, cover and simmer until just tender: 5–15 minutes according to the size of the pieces. *To braise*, cook grated celeriac, with 2 oz (55 g) butter and 2 tablespoons stock per 1 lb (450 g), covered, for 5 minutes. Uncover and boil to evaporate excess liquid.

Serving ideas (4–5 oz/115–145 g each)

- Dress matchsticks of celeriac with spicy mayonnaise and sprinkle with shredded salami.
- Boil slices of celeriac in beef stock; drain. Sprinkle with grated Parmesan cheese and serve hot.

Onions

The onion is one of those ingredients basic to almost every savoury dish. They come in all sizes and shapes: pungent round onions and sweet mild onions, flat ones, large spherical ones (Spanish-type) and elongated Italian red ones. In addition, there are small pickling and button onions, shallots and spring onions.

Preparation: Peel off the papery skin. Then slice, chop, etc as the recipe specifies. For spring onions, trim the root end and cut off any wilted or discoloured green leaves. Cut as specified, using just the white bulbs or both white and green parts.

Cooking: *To fry*, cook chopped or sliced onions, uncovered, in butter and/or oil over moderate heat, stirring occasionally, for about 5 minutes or until soft and translucent. If directed, continue cooking until the onions are golden brown. *To slow-cook*, cook sliced or chopped onions, covered, in butter and/or oil over low heat, stirring occasionally, for about 30 minutes or until very soft and golden. *To boil* small onions, drop into boiling salted water and simmer for 15–20 minutes or until tender.

Serving ideas

- Top hamburgers or steaks with slow-cooked sliced onions.
- Combine 1 lb (450 g) boiled button onions with 1½ oz (45 g) butter and 2½ oz (70 g) soft light brown sugar; cook over low heat, stirring, for about 10 minutes or until caramelized.
- Trim all but 2 in (5 cm) of green from spring onions. Stir-fry in hot oil and sprinkle with soy sauce.
- Use thin slices of sweet red onions raw in salads.
- Bake whole onions in a 425°F/ 220°C/Gas 7 oven for 45 minutes or until tender when pierced with a fork.

Leeks

This sweet and subtle member of the onion family has myriad uses – both as a vegetable on its own and as a flavouring in soups, stews and so on.

Preparation: Trim the root end and the dark green leaves, leaving just the pale green and white. (Save the dark green leaves for the stockpot.) Unless the leeks are to be cooked whole, slit them open lengthways, to the centre. Put them in cold water and soak for about 20 minutes. Drain well, squeezing out the excess water. If leeks are to be sliced or chopped, do this before rinsing them thoroughly in a colander under cold running water.

Cooking: *To braise*, cook, with 1 oz (30 g) butter and 5 tablespoons stock or water per 1 lb (450 g), tightly covered, until just tender. *To boil*, drop into boiling salted water or stock and simmer for 10–15 minutes or until tender. *To steam*, cook in a covered steamer over boiling water, allowing 5–7 minutes for sliced or whole baby leeks.

Serving ideas (6 oz/170 g each)
● Boil whole leeks, then cool slightly. Marinate in a vinaigrette dressing; serve the leeks cool, not cold.
● Toss hot sliced leeks with butter and fresh herbs such as sage, tarragon, thyme or parsley.
● Wrap whole boiled leeks in slices of ham. Cover with cheese sauce, sprinkle with grated cheese and grill until the top is golden.

FRUITING VEGETABLES
Aubergines
The most familiar aubergines are the large ones with shiny purple skins, but there are also smaller purple ones and long, pale purple Chinese ones. All can be used interchangeably.

Preparation: Trim off the stalk end. Leave aubergines whole or cut according to recipe instructions.

Cooking: *To grill*, brush cut surfaces with oil. Grill, 3–4 in (7.5–10 cm) from the heat, for 10 minutes or until tender and well browned; turn once and brush with oil. *To fry*, coat slices or thick sticks with flour if recipe specifies, then fry in hot oil or butter for 5 minutes on each side or until golden. *To braise* brown slices or wedges in a little hot oil, add 4 tablespoons stock or water per 1 lb (450 g), cover and cook for 12 minutes or until tender. Add more liquid if necessary. *To bake*, prick whole aubergines all over with a fork. Bake in a 400°F/200°C/Gas 6 oven for about 20 minutes or until soft.

Serving ideas (5 oz/145 g each)
● Baste grilled aubergines with garlic- and herb-flavoured olive oil.
● When braising aubergines, after browning add skinned, seeded and chopped tomatoes and basil.
● Serve fried flour-coated aubergines with garlic mayonnaise.

Courgettes
Courgettes and other thin-skinned squashes, such as pattypan, are completely edible, skin and all.

Preparation: Trim the ends from courgettes. Cut as specified.

Cooking: *To fry*, cook sliced courgettes in butter or oil for 5–10 minutes or until tender and golden brown. *To boil*, drop into boiling salted water and simmer until tender: 10–12 minutes for whole courgettes, 3–8 minutes for slices. *To steam*, cook in a covered steamer over boiling water until tender. *To braise*, cook sliced courgettes in a covered pan, with 1 oz (30 g) butter and 5 table- spoons stock or water per 1 lb (450 g), for 4–5 minutes or until tender.

Serving ideas (4–5 oz/115–145 g each)
● Sauté sliced courgettes with finely chopped garlic and chopped fresh parsley and oregano.
● Cut small courgettes in half lengthways and spread cut surfaces with wholegrain mustard. Grill about 4 in (10 cm) from the heat for about 5 minutes or until tender but still firm.

Pumpkins
Pumpkin and other squashes such as acorn and butternut, have a hard rind and central seeds and fibres that should be removed before cooking.

Preparation: Unless baking in the skin, peel pumpkin with a large, sturdy knife. Scrape away all the seeds and stringy fibres.

Cooking: *To steam,* cook in a covered steamer over boiling water until tender. *To bake,* cut into serving pieces, leaving on the rind, and score the flesh. Arrange cut side up in greased baking dish, dot with butter and bake in a 375°F/190°C/Gas 5 oven for 45 minutes or until tender. *To boil,* drop pieces into boiling salted water and simmer for 4–5 minutes or until tender. *To braise,* cook cubes of pumpkin as for courgettes.

Serving ideas (5–8 oz/145–225 g each)
● Add diced apple, a squeeze of lemon juice and 2 tablespoons soft brown sugar when braising pumpkin. If desired, spice with a little cinnamon and nutmeg or curry powder.
● Bake acorn squash halves with a knob of butter and 1 teaspoon maple syrup in each.

LEAFY, GREEN AND OTHER VEGETABLES

Spinach
Small tender leaves have a delicate flavour and can be used raw in salads. Large, strongly flavoured, darker leaves taste better cooked.

Preparation: Spinach can hide a lot of grit so needs careful rinsing. Immerse in cold water, swish round and soak

for 3–4 minutes. Then lift out the spinach and immerse in fresh cold water. Repeat, then drain in a colander. Discard any damaged or yellowed leaves. Pull off tough stalks.

Cooking: *To steam-boil,* put into a large pan (there should be sufficient water left on the leaves after rinsing so that no more is needed). Cook for 5–7 minutes or until just wilted, stirring occasionally to help evaporate the liquid. Drain well and press the spinach between two plates or squeeze it in your fist. *To braise,* cook, covered, with a large knob of butter until wilted. Uncover and boil to evaporate excess liquid. *To stir-fry,* cook small or shredded leaves in hot oil for 3–5 minutes or until wilted.

Serving ideas (5–6 oz/145–175 g each)
● Add 3–4 tablespoons double or whipping cream and a good pinch of grated nutmeg to braised spinach.
● Stir-fry chopped onion and garlic, then add spinach with halved cherry tomatoes and stir-fry for 1 minute.
● Steam-boil spinach leaves; chop finely after draining. Fry in olive oil with chopped garlic, stirring, until the garlic just starts to turn golden and the spinach is piping hot.
● Combine equal parts of chopped cooked spinach and cooked rice with butter and seasoning to taste.

Greens
Hearty greens include those from the cabbage family – kale, spring greens, turnip leaves – as well as beet greens and Swiss chard or seakale beet. Serve alone, or in soups and stews.

Preparation: Discard damaged or yellowed leaves. Trim off root ends and large or coarse stalks. Leave the leaves whole or shred, according to recipe instructions. Cut leaves from stalks of Swiss chard and cook separately (the stalks take longer).

Cooking: *To braise,* put shredded leaves (or Swiss chard stalks) in a pan, with 1 oz (30 g) butter and 3 tablespoons stock per 1 lb (450 g). Cook, covered, until just tender. Boil, uncovered, to evaporate excess liquid. *To steam-boil,* put into a large pan (there should be sufficient water left on the leaves after rinsing so that no more is needed). Cover and cook until just wilted: 5–15 minutes according to variety. *To boil,* drop shredded leaves (or Swiss chard stalks) into boiling salted water and simmer until tender.

Serving ideas (8 oz/225 g each)
● Toss hot braised greens with whipping cream or soured cream and grated nutmeg; heat gently.
● Mix boiled greens with mashed potato. Shape into cakes, coat in fine breadcrumbs and fry in butter until golden brown on both sides.
● Top boiled or braised greens with crisply fried bacon and grated Gruyère cheese; grill to melt the cheese.

Green beans

Crisp green beans are available in varying sizes, from tiny French ones ('haricots verts') to very large runner beans. French beans are stringless, whereas runner beans when mature have a stringy casing. Bobby beans are shorter and plumper than French beans. Chinese long beans are similar to runner beans, but longer.

Preparation: Top and tail using scissors or a knife. For older beans with strings, snap off the ends, pulling the strings from the sides as you do so. Cut large beans diagonally or sliver.

Cooking: *To boil,* drop into boiling salted water and simmer until just tender but still crisp and bright green: 3–15 minutes, according to size. *To steam,* cook in a covered steamer over boiling water until tender. *To braise,* cook tightly covered, with about 5 tablespoons stock or water and 1 oz (30 g) butter per 1 lb (450 g), until tender. *To stir-fry,* blanch in boiling water for 2 minutes; drain, refresh and dry. Stir-fry in hot oil for 2–3 minutes.

Serving ideas (4 oz/115 g each)
- Dress boiled or steamed beans with melted butter, chopped herbs and a squeeze of lemon juice.

- Add 6 tablespoons cream to 1 lb (450 g) braised beans. Cook, uncovered, stirring, until the liquid has reduced and the beans are glazed.
- Top hot beans with quickly fried shreds of Parma ham. Or, top with flaked almonds or pecan nuts lightly browned in butter.

Peas

Mange-touts and sugar-snap peas are completely edible, pod and all. Green peas are removed from their pods for cooking; the pods weigh as much as the peas, so you need to allow twice the weight of edible-pod peas.

Preparation: If green peas are in the pod, split it open and pop out the peas. Top and tail mange-touts and sugar-snap peas, pulling any tough strings from the sides as you do so.

Cooking: *To steam,* cook in a covered steamer over boiling water until tender. *To boil,* drop into boiling salted water and simmer until tender: 5–10 minutes for peas, 1–2 minutes for mange-touts. *To braise,* cook covered, with 1 oz (30 g) butter and 4 tablespoons stock or water per 1 lb (450 g), until tender: 5–10 minutes for green peas, 2 minutes for mange-touts and sugar-snap peas.

Serving ideas (4 oz/115 g each)
- Add sliced spring onions, shredded lettuce and a little sugar when braising green peas.
- Stir-fry mange-touts with thinly sliced onion and mushrooms.
- Add 4 tablespoons whipping cream to 1 lb (450 g) braised sugar-snap peas and cook uncovered, stirring, until almost all liquid has evaporated.

Broccoli

Serve this green vegetable hot or leave it to cool and use in salads. It is also excellent in stir-fries.

Preparation: Trim off the end of the stalk. If the rest of the stalk is to be used in the recipe, peel it. According to recipe instructions, leave the head whole or cut off the florets, or flowers, taking a little stalk with each one. Cut the remainder of the peeled stalk across into thin slices.

Cooking: *To steam,* cook in a covered steamer over boiling water until tender. *To boil,* drop into boiling salted water and simmer until just tender: 7–12 minutes for whole, 4–6 minutes for florets and stalks. *To braise,* cook covered, with 5 tablespoons stock or water and 1 oz (30 g) butter per 1 lb (450 g), until tender.

Serving ideas (5 oz/145 g each)
● Toss hot broccoli with a flavoured butter.
● Cover hot broccoli with cheese sauce, sprinkle with grated Parmesan and brown under grill.
● Blanch small broccoli florets for 1 minute; drain and refresh. Serve cold dressed with vinaigrette and sprinkled with toasted nuts.

Cauliflower

White or ivory cauliflower is the most widely available, although there are also green and purple varieties.

Preparation: Cut away the large green leaves, leaving only the tiny ones if liked. Trim the stalk level with the the head. Cut out the core. Leave the head whole, or break into florets before or after cooking.

Cooking: *To steam*, cook florets in a covered steamer over boiling water for 12–15 minutes. *To steam-boil*, put core down in a pan with 1 in (2.5 cm) boiling salted water and a bay leaf. Cover and cook until just tender: 15–30 minutes for whole heads, 5–9 minutes for florets. Drain well. *To braise*, cook florets, covered, with 1 oz (30 g) butter and 5 tablespoons stock or water per 1 lb (450 g), for 5–7 minutes.

Serving ideas (5 oz/145 g each)
● Dress hot cauliflower with butter; sprinkle with chopped fresh chives, toasted flaked almonds or chopped pecan nuts, or paprika.
● Top hot cauliflower with Hollandaise sauce.
● Coat florets in egg and crumbs, then deep-fry and serve with garlic or spicy mayonnaise.

Cabbage

Rich in vitamins and very versatile, cabbage is good cooked or raw. The many varieties available include firm, round heads (green, white and red), looser round heads (Savoy with its crinkly leaves), and long, loose heads (pak choi and Chinese leaves or Chinese cabbage).

Preparation: Discard any wilted or discoloured outer leaves. Cut the heads into small wedges or halve long, loose heads. Cut out the coarse stalk from the wedges before cooking, if preferred. Or, quarter heads and shred them. Leave long, loose heads whole and cut across the leaves to shred.

Cooking: *To braise*, quickly blanch chopped or shredded green, Savoy or red cabbage. (There is no need to blanch Chinese leaves.) Cook, tightly covered, with about 5 tablespoons stock or water and 1 oz (30 g) butter per 1 lb (450 g), allowing 3–4 minutes for green, Savoy and Chinese leaves and 30 minutes for red cabbage (use more liquid). *To boil*, drop into boiling salted water and simmer until just tender: 6–8 minutes for wedges and 3–5 minutes for shredded green, Savoy or Chinese leaves. *To steam*, cook in a covered steamer over boiling water until tender.

Serving ideas (4 oz/115 g each)
● Add chopped fresh dill when braising green or Savoy cabbage.
● Blanch larger outer leaves of green or Savoy cabbage, then roll them up around a minced meat stuffing and simmer in a rich tomato sauce.
● Add sliced apples, cooked diced bacon and spices (cinnamon, nutmeg) when braising red cabbage.
● Use shredded Chinese leaves raw in tossed salads.

Cauliflower Cheese
Cut a large cauliflower into florets and steam until just tender. Spread in a buttered gratin dish and scatter over 3 oz (85 g) sliced, sautéed mushrooms. Pour 1 pint (600 ml) cheese sauce evenly over the top and sprinkle with a mixture of grated Cheddar cheese and fine breadcrumbs. Brown quickly under the grill. *Serves 4.*

Brussels sprouts

These miniature heads of cabbage are best cooked just until tender.

Preparation: Remove any discoloured leaves. Trim the stalks level with the heads. Cut an 'x' in the base of the stalk so that it will cook in the same time as the rest.

Cooking: *To braise,* put in a pan, with 5 tablespoons stock or water and 1 oz (30 g) butter per 1 lb (450 g). Cover tightly for cooking. *To boil,* drop into boiling salted water and simmer for 7–10 minutes or until just tender. *To steam,* cook in a covered steamer over boiling water for 10–12 minutes.

Serving ideas (4–5 oz/115–145 g each)
- Toss with butter and orange zest.
- Toss with toasted nuts, braised or poached chestnuts or canned water chestnuts.
- Cut the heads lengthways in half and blanch in boiling water for 2–3 minutes; drain and refresh. Stir-fry in hot oil with finely chopped ginger and garlic for 2–3 minutes or until tender and lightly browned.
- Shred and blanch for 2–3 minutes; drain and refresh. Add chopped onion and celery and toss with a lemony vinaigrette dressing.

Celery

Crisp green or white celery is a popular salad ingredient and favourite flavouring in soups, stews and stuffings.

Preparation: Separate the stalks. Scrub with a vegetable brush under cold running water. Trim off the root end, leaves and any blemishes (keep leaves for the stockpot). If the stalks have tough strings, remove these with a vegetable peeler. Cut as specified. For celery hearts, cut in half lengthways. Trim off the leaves.

Cooking: *To steam-boil,* put in a pan with 1 in (2.5 cm) of boiling salted water. Cover and cook until just tender: 5–10 minutes for pieces, 10–20 minutes for celery hearts. *To braise,* cook slices, with 2 tablespoons stock or water and 1 oz (30 g) butter per 8 oz (225 g), or hearts with ½ pint (300 ml) liquid, covered: about 3 minutes for thin slices 10–20 minutes for hearts.

Serving ideas (4 oz/115 g each)
- Stuff finger-length sticks of raw celery with blue cheese, flavoured soft cheese or peanut butter.
- Sprinkle braised celery with chopped walnuts and chopped parsley.
- Braise celery hearts with chopped tomatoes and tarragon or thyme.

Mushrooms

Cultivated button and open mushrooms are widely available; you may also find fresh wild mushrooms such as shiitake and oyster.

Preparation: Rinse or wipe with a damp paper towel (don't immerse in water as mushrooms absorb liquid readily). Trim gritty stalks, and remove tough stalks from wild mushrooms. Small mushrooms can be left whole; larger ones are normally halved, quartered or sliced, or they may be diced or chopped. To stuff large mushrooms, pull off the stalks.

Cooking: *To fry,* cook in hot butter and/or oil for about 4 minutes or until tender, stirring frequently. The mushrooms will give up liquid; if the recipe specifies, continue frying until the liquid has evaporated and the mushrooms have browned. *To grill,* brush with melted butter or oil. Grill 4 in (10 cm) from the heat, turning and basting occasionally, for 5–8 minutes or until tender and browned.

Serving ideas (4 oz/115 g each)
- Sauté sliced mushrooms with chopped garlic and thyme.
- Top grilled mushroom caps with a pat of flavoured butter.

CHOPPING VEGETABLES

In countless recipes, vegetables and other ingredients are required to be chopped to varying degrees of fineness. For most chopping, a large chef's knife should be used (be sure it is sharp). You can also use a food processor, but take care not to over-process the vegetables to a pulp.

Cheese and Herb Dip
Combine 8 oz (225 g) each full-fat soft cheese and cottage cheese in a food processor or blender and blend until smooth. Turn into a bowl and stir in 2 tablespoons chopped fresh dill and ¾ oz (25 g) chopped chives. Season to taste with salt and pepper. If the dip is too thick, stir in a few spoonfuls of cream or milk. Cover and chill for at least 1 hour before serving, with crudités, savoury biscuits and crisps for dipping. *Makes about 1 lb (450 g)*.

Peeling whole garlic
If you want to peel garlic and keep the clove whole, drop it into boiling water, count to 30, then drain and rinse with cold water. The skin will slip off easily.

1 ▲ To chop an onion: Peel it, leaving on the root end to hold the onion together. Cut it in half, straight through the root.

3 ▲ Make vertical lengthways cuts in the onion half, again not cutting the root. Then, cut across the onion to chop it, guiding the side of the knife with your knuckles. Discard the root.

5 ▲ Crush the peeled clove again with the knife to flatten it, then begin to chop it. When it is coarsely chopped, continue chopping and crushing it until it is almost a paste. Hold the tip of the knife on the board and raise and lower the knife handle with your other hand, moving the blade back and forth over the garlic.

2 ▲ Put one half flat on the work surface and hold the onion steady at the root end. With a chef's knife, make horizontal cuts in the onion half, to the root but without cutting all the way through it.

4 ▲ To chop garlic finely: Set a chef's knife flat on top of the clove and bang it gently with the side of your fist to crush the garlic slightly and loosen the peel. Remove the peel.

6 ▲ To chop fresh herbs: Hold the leaves or sprigs together in a bunch and chop coarsely, then continue chopping as for garlic (without crushing). You can also use this method of fine chopping for vegetables and fresh root ginger.

BLANCHING AND REFRESHING

Foods are blanched for several reasons: to loosen skins before skinning (tomatoes, peaches and nuts), to set colour and flavour (for vegetables before freezing), to reduce bitterness (in some vegetables), to firm flesh (sweetbreads), and to remove excess salt (gammon, bacon). Vegetables are often blanched as an initial cooking, when further cooking is to be done by stir-frying or a brief reheating in butter before serving, or if they are to be used in a salad. After blanching, most foods are 'refreshed' to stop them cooking any further.

1 ▲ **To blanch:** Immerse the food in a large pan of boiling water (ideally use a wire basket or sieve so the food can be lifted out easily). Bring the water back to the boil and boil for the time specified, usually 1–2 minutes. Immediately lift the food out of the water (in its basket or with a slotted spoon, or drain in a colander).

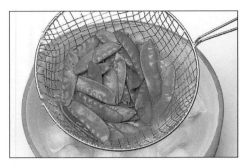

2 ▲ **To refresh:** Quickly immerse the food in iced water or hold under cold running water. If the recipe specifies, leave until it has cooled completely. Drain well.

Broccoli, Cauliflower and Carrot Salad

SERVES 4

1 small cauliflower, cut into florets and stalks trimmed

8 oz (225 g) broccoli, cut into florets and stalks trimmed

2 carrots, thickly sliced

5 tablespoons vegetable oil

3 tablespoons chopped almonds

2 tablespoons red wine vinegar

½ teaspoon ground cumin

salt and pepper

1 Blanch the cauliflower, broccoli and carrots separately in boiling salted water, allowing 10 minutes for the cauliflower and 5 minutes for the broccoli and carrots. Drain well and refresh in iced water.

2 ▶ Heat 1 tablespoon of the oil in a small frying pan. Add the almonds. Fry for about 5 minutes or until golden brown, stirring frequently. Drain on paper towels and leave to cool.

3 Combine the remaining oil with the vinegar, cumin, salt and pepper in a large bowl. Whisk well together. Add the vegetables and toss to coat with the dressing. Scatter the almonds on top. Serve at room temperature.

SWEATING

Sweating is a common preliminary step in vegetable cooking, particularly for onions and leeks. This process, which is essentially a form of steaming, draws out the juices and develops the vegetable's flavour.

A matter of weight
Be sure the pan you use for sweating has a heavy base that will conduct the heat evenly, so the vegetables don't stick and burn. It is also important that the lid be tight fitting to keep in moisture.

1 ▲ Heat fat (usually butter) in a heavy saucepan or frying pan over low heat. Add the vegetable and stir to coat with the melted fat.

2 ▲ Cover the pan tightly and cook gently until the vegetable is softened but not brown; onions will be translucent. This can take 10–15 minutes or longer. Stir occasionally during the cooking.

Pasta with Courgette and Walnut Sauce

SERVES 4

2 ½ oz (70 g) butter

1 large Spanish-type onion, halved and thinly sliced

1 lb (450 g) courgettes, very thinly sliced

12 oz (340 g) short pasta shapes such as penne, ziti, rotini or fusilli

2 oz (55 g) walnuts, coarsely chopped

3 tablespoons chopped fresh parsley

2 tablespoons single cream

salt and pepper

freshly grated Parmesan cheese, to serve

1 ▲ Melt the butter in a frying pan. Add the onion, cover and sweat for 5 minutes, then add the courgettes.

2 Stir well, cover again and sweat until the vegetables are very soft, stirring occasionally.

3 Meanwhile, bring a large pot of salted water to the boil. Add the pasta to the boiling water, stir and cook for 10 minutes or until it is just tender to the bite ('al dente'). Check the packet instructions for timing.

4 While the pasta is cooking, add the walnuts, parsley and cream to the courgette mixture and stir well. Season with salt and pepper.

5 Drain the pasta and return it to the pot. Add the courgette sauce and mix well together. Serve immediately, with freshly grated Parmesan to sprinkle on top of each portion.

MASHING AND PURÉEING

The smooth texture of a mashed or puréed vegetable is very appealing, perhaps because it reminds us of nursery food. Vegetables to be finished this way may be first boiled, steamed, sweated or baked.

Carrot Purée
Thinly slice 1½ lb (700 g) carrots. Put them in a saucepan, cover with water and add a pinch of salt. Bring to the boil and simmer for 10–15 minutes or until tender. Drain well, then purée in a food processor. Add 1 oz (30 g) butter, 4 tablespoons each milk and orange juice, and ½ teaspoon ground cardamom or a pinch of grated nutmeg. Season with salt and pepper. Reheat, stirring frequently. *Serves 4.*

Sweet Potato Purée
Mash 1½ lb (700 g) boiled or baked sweet potatoes with an electric mixer. Beat in butter, 4 tablespoons orange juice and ¼ teaspoon ground cinnamon.

1 ▲ To mash potatoes and sweet potatoes: Mash warm, freshly cooked potatoes with a potato masher or put them through a potato ricer. With a wooden spoon, beat in butter and milk or cream, and season to taste.

3 ▲ To purée other root vegetables or pumpkin: Put the freshly cooked vegetable in a food processor and process until smooth, scraping down the sides of the container as necessary. Season to taste.

2 ▲ Alternatively, beat the potatoes with an electric mixer. Do not use a food processor for puréeing starchy vegetables such as potatoes because it will make them gluey.

4 ▲ To purée vegetables with fibres or skins (such as asparagus or pulses): Use a vegetable mill, unless you are prepared to push the food-processor purée through a sieve.

5 ◄ To purée greens: Remove the stalks of leaves such as spinach or chard before cooking. Purée in a food processor. Be sure to squeeze out as much water as possible, both before and after puréeing, especially if adding cream.

MAKING VEGETABLE STOCK

Vary the ingredients for this fresh-flavoured stock according to what you have to hand. Refrigerate, covered, for up to 5 days; freeze up to 1 month.

MAKES ABOUT 4 PINTS (2.5 LITRES)

2 large onions, coarsely chopped

2 leeks, sliced

3 garlic cloves, crushed with the flat side of a knife

3 carrots, coarsely chopped

4 celery stalks, coarsely chopped

a large strip of lemon zest

a handful of parsley stalks (about 12)

a few fresh thyme sprigs

2 bay leaves

4 pints (2.5 litres) water

1 ▲ Put the vegetables, lemon zest, herbs and water in a stockpot and bring to the boil. Skim off the foam that rises to the surface, frequently at first and then from time to time.

2 ▲ Reduce the heat and simmer, uncovered, for 30 minutes. Strain the stock and leave it to cool.

Vegetable and Herb Chowder

SERVES 4

1 oz (30 g) butter

1 onion, finely chopped

1 leek, thinly sliced

1 celery stalk, diced

1 pepper, yellow or green, seeded and diced

2 tablespoons chopped fresh parsley

1 tablespoon plain flour

2 pints (1.2 litres) vegetable stock

12 oz (340 g) boiling potatoes, peeled and diced

a few fresh thyme sprigs or ½ teaspoon dried thyme

1 bay leaf

4 oz (115 g) young runner beans, thinly sliced on the diagonal

4 fl oz (120 ml) milk

salt and pepper

1 ▲ Melt the butter in a heavy saucepan or flameproof casserole and add the onion, leek, celery, pepper and parsley. Cover and cook over low heat until the vegetables are soft.

2 Add the flour and stir until well blended. Add the stock slowly, stirring to combine. Bring to the boil, stirring frequently.

3 ▼ Add the potatoes, thyme and bay leaf. Simmer, uncovered, for about 10 minutes.

4 Add the beans and simmer for a further 10–15 minutes or until all the vegetables are tender.

5 Stir in the milk. Season with salt and pepper. Heat through. Before serving, discard the thyme stalks and bay leaf. Serve hot.

PREPARING SALAD GREENS

Crisp, fresh green and variegated leaves are very appetizing. Use them as the background for a vegetable, fish, meat or fruit salad or make the leaves the focus.

Lettuce

The four main types are: crisphead, with solid heads of tightly packed, crisp leaves (iceberg); butterhead, with looser heads of soft-textured leaves (round, 'quattro stagioni'); Cos and romaine, with elongated heads of crisp leaves; and looseleaf, with leaves that do not form a compact head ('feuilles de chêne', 'lollo rosso').

Preparation: Discard wilted or damaged leaves. Twist or cut out the central core. Rinse the leaves thoroughly in cold water and soak briefly to draw out any grit trapped in the folds. Drain and blot or spin dry. If the leaves are large, tear into pieces.

Other salad ingredients

To provide contrast in texture and flavour, add brightly coloured and crunchy leaves, such as red cabbage, with plain salad leaves – just a little goes a long way. Cucumber, spring onions and carrot are also appealing in a mixed salad, as are raw or lightly cooked French beans or mangetouts. Nuts or dried fruit are other tasty additions.

Chicory and Endive

These have an appealing bitterness. Paler leaves are more delicate and sweet. 'Frisée' or curly endive has fine, frilly green leaves with a coarse texture. Escarole has broader, fleshier leaves with jagged edges and a firm texture. The slim leaves of chicory are white with greenish tips. Radicchio is red Italian chicory.

Preparation: Core the base of chicory. Discard wilted or damaged leaves. Rinse thoroughly and dry the leaves. If large, cut into pieces.

Lamb's Lettuce

Also known as corn salad or 'mâche', this salad green has a pleasantly firm, chewy texture and mild, slightly nutty flavour. The leaves are small and may be spoon-shaped or round.

Preparation: Remove any wilted or damaged leaves. Trim roots. Rinse well as the leaves can be sandy.

Rocket

In a salad of mixed greens, the pungent peppery, nutty taste of rocket is unmistakable and welcome. This member of the mustard family, also called 'roquette' and 'arugula', has deep green leaves with curved edges and a texture somewhat like spinach.

Preparation: Discard any wilted or damaged leaves. Pull off roots. Rinse thoroughly and dry on paper towels – it's best not to use a salad spinner, which could bruise the tender leaves.

Watercress

Another member of the mustard family, the round dark green leaves have a wonderful peppery flavour that enlivens any salad, and the fresh attractive appearance of watercress makes it a popular garnish.

Preparation: Discard wilted or damaged leaves and snap off thick stalks. Rinse well and spin dry.

RINSING AND CRISPING SALAD GREENS

It is vital that all salad leaves be thoroughly rinsed with cold water to remove any grit or insects, as well as residues of sprays. Just as important is to dry the salad leaves well so that the dressing will not be diluted.

Lettuce with Blue Cheese Dressing

For each serving, use 1 small head round lettuce or Little Gem lettuce, washed and spun or blotted dry. Top with 3–4 tablespoons of a blue cheese dressing. Garnish with cherry tomatoes and chives, if you like.

Salad success

● Dress salad greens just before serving, otherwise the leaves will wilt and become unpleasantly soggy.

● Match the dressing to the greens: sharp leaves need hearty flavours, but the same dressing used on delicate greens would overpower them.

● Be imaginative with salad additions. A few blanched French beans, for instance, can lift a plain salad, especially with a sprinkling of fresh herbs.

1 ▲ Discard any wilted, discoloured or damaged leaves. For spinach and similar greens, pull off the stalks. Pull off roots from lamb's lettuce.

3 ▲ Put the leaves in a sink or large basin of cold water and swirl them round to wash off any dirt or insects. Leave to settle for 1–2 minutes.

5 ▲ Alternatively, put the washed leaves in a salad spinner to spin off the water. (Do not use a salad spinner for leaves that bruise easily.)

2 ▲ For leaves in compact or loose heads pull them individually from the core or stalk.

4 ▲ Lift the leaves out of the water on to a tea towel and pat dry gently with paper towels or another tea towel.

6 ▲ Wrap the leaves loosely in a clean tea towel or paper towels and put in a large plastic bag. Refrigerate for about 1 hour. When assembling the salad, tear any large leaves into smaller pieces.

Eggs

~

Eggs are so versatile, and this chapter shows how to make perfect boiled, scrambled, fried, baked and poached eggs, as well as describing techniques for turning eggs into batters and pancake mixtures.

BOILING EGGS

The derisive expression, 'can't boil an egg', indicates the importance of this basic cooking skill, although, to be accurate, eggs are simmered rather than boiled.

For many people, a boiled egg with toast is an everyday breakfast. But the soft-boiled egg and its cousin the coddled egg have many delicious applications. If they are to be peeled for serving, cook them for the longest time suggested below. The salt in the cooking water aids in peeling.

Hard-boiled eggs make classic salads and sandwich fillings, as well as cold first course and buffet dishes and hot main dishes.

1 ▲ To hard-boil eggs: Bring a pan of well-salted water to the boil. Using a slotted spoon, lower each egg into the water. Reduce the heat so the water is just simmering. Cook for 10 minutes. Immediately plunge the eggs into a bowl of iced water to cool.

2 ▲ When the eggs are cool enough to handle, peel them. If they are not to be used immediately, keep the peeled eggs in a bowl of cold salted water. Or store the eggs, still in the shell, in the refrigerator; they will keep for up to 1 week.

Egg, Potato and Bean Salad
Bring a pot of salted water to the boil. Add 1 lb (450 g) small un-peeled new potatoes. Bring back to the boil and simmer for 10 minutes. Add 8 oz (225 g) French beans and simmer for 4–5 minutes or until the potatoes and beans are just tender. Drain well in a colander and refresh under cold running water. Turn the vegetables into a large bowl. Sprinkle 4 tablespoons olive oil and 2 tablespoons balsamic vinegar over them. Season with salt and pepper and toss well. Scatter 2 grated hard-boiled eggs and 3 tablespoons coarsely shredded mixed fresh mint and basil over the top. Serve warm or at room temperature. *Serves 4–6.*

3 ▲ To coddle eggs: Lower them into a pan of boiling salted water. Cover the pan and remove it from the heat. Leave for 6–8 minutes or until the eggs are done to your taste. Lift out each egg, place in an egg cup and cut off the top of the shell for serving. Or, to peel, plunge the eggs into a bowl of cold water. When they are cool enough to handle, peel carefully. To reheat for serving, immerse in a bowl of hot water for 1–2 minutes.

Hard-boiled egg tips
● Always cool hard-boiled eggs in iced water. The abrupt temperature change helps prevent a grey layer from forming round the yolk.
● To peel hard-boiled eggs, tap them gently on a hard surface to crack the shell. Carefully peel under cold running water.

4 ▲ To soft-boil eggs: Bring a pan of well-salted water to the boil. Using a slotted spoon, lower each egg into the water. Reduce the heat so the water just simmers. Cook for 3–5 minutes or until the eggs are done to your taste (depending on how firm you like the white; the yolk will be runny).

Ideas for soft-boiled and coddled eggs
● For *Caviar-crowned Eggs*: Cut the top ¾ in (2 cm) from each egg, in its shell. Put a spoonful of soured cream and caviar on top.
● For *Smoked Salmon Eggs*: Prepare as above and top each with a spoonful each of soured cream and diced smoked salmon.
● Put a hot peeled egg in the centre of a bowl of cream of spinach or watercress soup.

Scrambling Eggs

Tender, creamy scrambled eggs are perfect for breakfast or brunch, but you can also add flavourings for a more unusual snack or supper dish.

<table>
<tr><td>

Ideas for scrambled eggs
- Add chopped fresh herbs (chives, tarragon) to the eggs.
- Cook diced vegetables (onions, mushrooms, peppers) or ham in butter before adding the eggs.
- Stir in a little grated cheese or bits of full-fat soft cheese just before the eggs are ready.
- Fold peeled cooked prawns into scrambled eggs.

</td></tr>
</table>

1 ▲ Put the eggs in a bowl and add a little salt and pepper. Beat the eggs with a fork until they are well blended. Melt butter in a frying pan over moderately low heat (it should cover the bottom of the pan generously). Pour in the beaten eggs.

2 ▲ Cook, scraping up and turning the eggs over, for 3–5 minutes or until they are softly set and still moist. The eggs will continue to cook after being removed from the heat, so undercook them slightly even if you prefer a firmer end result.

Scrambled Eggs with Smoked Salmon

Serves 4 as a snack

6 eggs

salt and pepper

2 oz (55 g) butter

2 tablespoons whipping cream

4 tablespoons mayonnaise

4 slices of pumpernickel or wholemeal bread, crusts trimmed

4 oz (115 g) thinly sliced smoked salmon

lumpfish or salmon caviar, to garnish

1 ▲ Season the eggs with salt and pepper. Scramble them using half of the butter. Mix in the cream just before they have finished cooking.

2 Remove from the heat and mix in the mayonnaise. Leave to cool.

3 Spread the slices of bread with the remaining butter. Cover with smoked salmon, trimming it to fit. Cut in half.

4 Divide the scrambled eggs among the plates, spreading it neatly on the smoked salmon. Top each serving with a heaped tablespoon of caviar.

FRYING EGGS

Fried eggs are a natural partner for bacon, sausages, fried tomatoes and mushrooms, and even black pudding in that great British institution – the 'cooked breakfast'.

1 Heat butter, bacon fat or oil (to generously cover the bottom) in a frying pan over moderate heat. When the fat is sizzling, break each egg and slip it into the pan.

2 ◀ Fry for 1–1½ minutes or until the egg white is just set and opaque or more firm, according to your taste. The yolk will still be runny and the base of the egg will be golden brown and crisp. The egg is ready to serve now, 'sunny side up'. Or gently turn the fried egg over with a fish slice, taking care not to break the yolk. Cook for a further 10–15 seconds or until the other side is just browned.

Fried Eggs and Sausage on Tortillas

SERVES 4

8 oz (225 g) minced pork

½ small onion, finely chopped

1 teaspoon chilli powder (or to taste)

½ teaspoon ground cumin

½ teaspoon dried oregano

1 tablespoon vinegar

1 garlic clove, finely chopped

salt and pepper

oil, for frying

4 large fresh or canned corn tortillas

4 eggs

2 oz (55 g) butter or bacon fat

Mexican hot sauce or salsa, to serve

1 ▲ Put the pork in a bowl and add the onion, spices, oregano, vinegar, garlic, salt and pepper. Mix well, cover and refrigerate overnight.

2 ▼ Cook the pork mixture in a large frying pan until it is browned and crumbly, stirring occasionally.

3 Meanwhile, heat 1 in (2.5 cm) oil in a wide pan to 365°F (180°C). Fry the tortillas until they are crisp and golden brown, keeping them flat. Drain on paper towels and put on a baking sheet. Keep warm in the oven.

4 Fry the eggs in the butter or bacon fat (or use oil for frying if you prefer).

5 Put a tortilla on each plate. Using a slotted spoon, divide the pork mixture among the tortillas. Top each serving with a fried egg. Serve with hot sauce or salsa.

BAKING EGGS

Baking is one of the simplest ways to cook eggs, yet it produces elegant results. The eggs can be baked individually, in buttered pots such as ramekins or small shallow dishes, or several can be baked in a large dish, on a bed of vegetables, sauce, etc.

1 ▲ To bake in individual ramekins: Butter the dishes and sprinkle them with salt and pepper. Break an egg into each, taking care not to pierce the yolk.

2 ▲ Dot the top of each egg with a few small pieces of butter, or add 1 tablespoon of whipping cream to each ramekin.

3 ▲ Set the dishes in a baking tin. Add enough water to come halfway up the sides of the dishes. Bring to a simmer on top of the stove. Transfer to a 400°F/200°C/Gas 6 oven. Bake for 5–7 minutes or until the whites are just set and the yolks still soft.

4 ▲ To bake on a bed: Spread a hot savoury mixture in a buttered shallow baking dish or in individual ramekins or gratin dishes. Make hollows in the mixture with the back of a spoon. Break an egg into each hollow.

5 ◄ According to recipe instructions, dot the eggs with butter, sprinkle with cheese, drizzle with cream, etc. These toppings help to prevent the eggs from drying out during cooking. Bake until the whites are just set and the yolks are still soft.

Ideas for baked eggs

● Coat buttered ramekins with freshly grated Parmesan cheese. Dot eggs with butter and sprinkle each egg very lightly with Parmesan before baking.

● Put a little diced cooked ham, or a few sautéed sliced mushrooms or crisp garlic-flavoured croutons in the bottom of each buttered ramekin before breaking in the egg.

● Bake eggs on a bed of creamed spinach, mashed potato or other root vegetables, puréed broccoli or peas.

● Bake eggs on tomato sauce and roasted vegetables.

● Bake eggs in hollows made in a cooked stuffing, such as sausage stuffing for chicken or smoked ham and almond stuffing for turkey.

● Bake potatoes, then cut off a lengthways slice from one side. Scoop out the flesh, leaving a shell ⅛–¼ in (3–5 mm) thick. Mash the potato with butter, milk, salt and pepper. Spoon it back into the potato shells and press down firmly. Make a hollow in the top of the mashed potato in each shell and break in an egg. Dribble a little melted butter over the egg. Bake at 400°F/200°C/Gas 6 for 5–7 minutes to set the egg white.

POACHING EGGS

The perfect poached egg has a neat oval shape, a tender white and a soft yolk. It is unbeatable on a slice of hot buttered toast, or it can be partnered with vegetables (artichoke hearts, asparagus), seafood (crab, smoked salmon) or meat (ham, bacon, steak) and dressed with a rich sauce. Use the freshest eggs possible because they will be the easiest to poach.

1 First, bring a large deep pan of water to the boil.

2 ▲ Break each egg and slip it gently into the water. Reduce the heat to low so the water just simmers. Poach for 3–4 minutes or until the eggs are done.

3 ▲ With a slotted spoon, lift out each egg and press it gently; the white should feel just firm but the yolk should still be soft.

The clotting factor

If your eggs are not really fresh, adding white wine vinegar to the poaching water will help the egg white to coagulate, although it will slightly flavour the egg. Use 2 tablespoons vinegar to 2 pints (1 litre) of water.

---

4 ◄ If there are any strings of cooked egg white, trim them off with a knife or kitchen scissors. Drain briefly on paper towels. Serve immediately, if wished. Or warm the eggs in a bowl of hot water for serving. If the eggs will be served cold, immerse them in a bowl of iced water until ready to serve. Drain and blot dry gently before serving.

Poached Eggs Florentine

SERVES 4

1½ lb (700 g) spinach leaves, shredded

1 oz (30 g) butter

3–4 tablespoons whipping cream

good pinch of grated nutmeg

salt and pepper

4 eggs

½ pint (300 ml) cheese sauce made with Gruyère cheese

1 oz (30 g) Gruyère cheese, grated

1 Preheat the grill.

2 Put the spinach in a large pan with the butter. Cover and cook until the leaves are wilted. Uncover and boil to evaporate the excess liquid.

3 ▲ Mix in the cream, nutmeg and seasoning. Poach the eggs.

4 Divide the spinach among 4 individual shallow gratin dishes or a large gratin dish. Spread it evenly and make hollows for the eggs. Set a poached egg in each hollow.

5 ▼ Spoon over cheese sauce to coat the eggs lightly. Sprinkle the grated cheese evenly over the top. Grill for 2–3 minutes or until the cheese has melted and is lightly browned. Serve immediately.

MAKING A ROLLED OMELETTE

The versatile rolled or folded omelette can be served plain or filled. There are also flat omelettes and soufflé omelettes. At its simplest, an omelette is made with 2 or 3 eggs, 1–2 teaspoons water, salt and pepper.

Ideas for omelettes
- Add 1 tablespoon chopped fresh herbs (a mixture of parsley, chives and tarragon, for example) to the beaten eggs.
- Scatter 2–3 tablespoons grated cheese (Gruyère, Cheddar) over the omelette before folding it.
- Sauté skinned, seeded and chopped tomatoes in butter for 1–2 minutes. Season with salt and pepper and stir in a little chopped fresh basil. Use this mixture to fill the omelette.
- Fill the omelette with thinly sliced strips of cooked ham or with Parma ham, roasted vegetables, sautéed sliced mushrooms, sautéed potatoes, buttered asparagus tips or slow-cooked onions.
- Warm left-over pasta (buttered or in sauce); if the shape is long, such as spaghetti, cut it into short pieces. If using buttered pasta, add strips of canned pimiento, sliced black olives, capers etc. Use to fill the omelette, fold and sprinkle with grated Parmesan.

The right pan
Although you can use a frying pan, a special omelette pan, with its curved edge, will make folding and turning out the omelette so much easier.

1 ▲ Break the eggs into a bowl and add the water and some salt and pepper. Beat with a fork until just blended but not frothy.

3 ▲ When the butter is foaming and just beginning to turn golden, pour in the egg mixture. Tilt and rotate the pan to spread the eggs in an even layer over the bottom.

5 ▲ With the palette knife, loosen the edge of the omelette on one side and tilt the pan so that a third of the omelette folds over on to itself.

2 ▲ In an 8 in (20 cm) omelette pan, melt a knob of butter over moderately high heat. Tilt and rotate the pan so the bottom and sides are thoroughly coated with butter.

4 ▲ Cook for 5–10 seconds or until the omelette starts to set on the base. With a palette knife, lift the cooked base and tilt the pan so the uncooked egg mixture runs underneath on to the hot pan. Continue cooking in this way until most of the omelette is set but the top is still moist and creamy.

6 ▲ Continue loosening the omelette from its folded edge, holding the pan over a warmed plate. As the omelette slides out on to the plate, tilt the pan so the omelette folds over again on itself into thirds, using the edge of the pan to guide it.

MAKING CUSTARD

A home-made custard is a luscious sauce for many hot and cold puddings. It is also the basis for a very rich ice cream, which is essentially a frozen custard enriched with cream.

The secret for success is patience. Don't try to hurry the cooking of the custard by raising the heat.

MAKES ABOUT ¾ PINT (450 ML)

¾ pint (450 ml) milk

1 vanilla pod, split in half

4 egg yolks

3–4 tablespoons caster sugar, to sprinkle

1 ▲ Put the milk in a heavy-based saucepan. Hold the vanilla pod over the pan and scrape out the tiny black seeds into the milk. Add the split pod to the milk.

2 ▲ Heat the milk until bubbles appear round the edge. Remove from the heat, cover and set aside to infuse for 10 minutes. Remove the split vanilla pod.

Custard variations

• Use 1 teaspoon vanilla essence instead of the vanilla pod. Omit steps 1 and 2, and add the essence after straining the custard.

• For *Chocolate Custard:* Add 2 oz (55 g) plain chocolate, grated, to the hot milk and sugar mixture. Stir until smooth before adding to the egg yolks.

• For *Mocha Custard:* Add 2 oz (55 g) plain chocolate, grated, and 2 teaspoons instant coffee powder or granules.

• For *Orange Custard:* Omit the vanilla pod and instead infuse the milk with the finely pared zest of 1 orange.

• For *Liqueur Custard:* Add 2–3 tablespoons brandy, kirsch or other liqueur to the custard.

Damage repair

If the custard gets too hot and starts to curdle, remove it from the heat immediately and pour it into a bowl. Whisk vigorously for 2–3 seconds or until smooth. Then pour it back into the pan and continue cooking.

3 ▲ In a bowl, lightly beat the egg yolks with the sugar until smoothly blended and creamy. Gradually add the hot milk to the egg yolks, stirring constantly

4 ▲ Pour the mixture into the top of a double saucepan (or a bowl). Set over the bottom pan containing hot water. Put on a moderately low heat, so the water stays below the boil.

5 ▲ Cook, stirring constantly, for 10–12 minutes or until the custard thickens to a creamy consistency that coats the spoon. Immediately remove the pan of custard from over the pan of hot water.

6 ▲ Strain the custard into a bowl. If using cold, sprinkle a little caster sugar over the surface of the custard to help prevent a skin from forming. Set the bowl in a container of iced water and leave to cool.

MAKING A BATTER

Batters consist mainly of flour, eggs and liquid. They may be thick – for making fritters or coating food to be fried – or thin and pourable, for Yorkshire pudding, or other batter puddings, and pancakes. For a very light result, the eggs can be separated and the whites whisked and folded in.

Pork and Apple Batter Puddings
Make the batter with 4 oz (115 g) plain flour, a pinch of salt, 1 egg and ½ pint (300 ml) mixed milk and water. Mix together 1 lb (450 g) pork sausagemeat, 4 oz (115 g) finely chopped or coarsely grated cooking apple, 1 small grated onion, 1 tablespoon chopped fresh parsley, salt and pepper. Form into 16 small balls. Oil 4 individual 1 pint (600 ml) baking dishes and heat in a 425°F/220°C/Gas 7 oven. Divide the balls among the dishes and bake for 10 minutes. Pour the batter over the balls and bake for 35–40 minutes or until risen and golden brown. Serve hot. *Serves 4.*

A speedy tip
Most batters can be made quickly in a blender or food processor. But take care not to overmix.

1 ▲ Sift the flour into a bowl along with other dry ingredients such as sugar, baking powder or bicarbonate of soda, salt, ground spices etc.

3 ▲ With a wooden spoon, beat together the eggs and liquid in the well just to mix them.

5 ▲ When the mixture is smooth, stir in the remaining liquid. Stir just until the ingredients are combined – the trick is not to overmix.

2 ▲ Make a well in the centre of the dry ingredients and put in the eggs or egg yolks and some of the liquid.

4 ▲ Gradually draw in some of the flour from the sides, stirring vigorously.

6 ▲ If the recipe specifies, whisk egg whites to a soft peak and fold them into the batter (made with yolks). Do this just before using the batter.

MAKING PANCAKES

Thin, lacy pancakes, or crêpes, are wonderfully versatile. They can be served very simply with just lemon juice and sugar, or turned into more elaborate dishes: folded and warmed in a sauce, rolled round a savoury or sweet filling, or stacked in layers with a filling.

MAKES ABOUT 12

6 oz (170 g) plain flour

2 teaspoons caster sugar (for sweet pancakes)

2 eggs

¾ pint (450 ml) milk

about 1 oz (30 g) melted butter

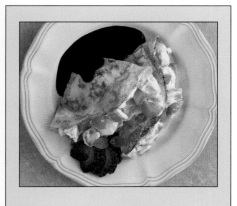

Ricotta and Peach Pancakes
Combine 1 lb (450 g) ricotta cheese, 1 oz (30 g) icing sugar, 1 teaspoon vanilla essence and 2 tablespoons brandy in a bowl. Mix well. Add 4 large ripe peaches, peeled and diced, and fold in gently. Divide the ricotta and peach mixture among 12 pancakes and spread it evenly over them. Fold each pancake in half and then in half again, into quarters. Arrange the pancakes in a buttered large oval baking dish, slightly overlapping them. Brush with 1 oz (30 g) melted butter and sprinkle generously with icing sugar. Bake in a 375°F/190°C/Gas 5 oven for 10 minutes. Serve hot, with a berry sauce if you wish. *Serves 6.*

1 ▲ Make the pancake batter and leave to stand for 20 minutes. Heat an 8 in (20 cm) pancake pan over moderate heat. The pan is ready when a few drops of water sprinkled on the surface jump and sizzle immediately. Grease the pan lightly with a little melted butter. Pour 3–4 tablespoons batter into the pan. Quickly tilt and rotate the pan so the batter spreads out to cover the bottom thinly and evenly; pour out any excess batter.

3 ▲ **To fill pancakes:** For folded pancakes, spread 3–4 tablespoons of filling evenly over each pancake. Fold in half then in half again, into quarters. For rolled pancakes, put 3–4 tablespoons of filling near one edge of each pancake and roll up tightly from that side. For pancake parcels, spoon 3–4 tablespoons of filling in the centre of each pancake. Fold in two opposite sides, over the filling, then fold in the other two sides. Turn the parcel over for serving. Filled pancakes are usually baked before serving, to reheat them.

2 ▲ Cook for 30–45 seconds or until the pancake is set and small holes have appeared. If the cooking seems to be taking too long, increase the heat slightly. Lift the edge of the pancake with a palette knife; the base of the pancake should be lightly brown. Shake the pan vigorously back and forth to loosen the pancake completely, then turn or flip it over. Cook the other side for about 30 seconds. Serve or leave to cool.

Pancake-making tips
- Pancake batter should be the consistency of whipping cream. If the batter is at all lumpy, strain it. If it doesn't flow smoothly to make a thin pancake, add a little more liquid.
- Like most batters, pancake batter can be made in a blender or food processor. It must have time to stand before using, as more air is incorporated by this method.
- Your first pancake may well be unsuccessful because it will test the consistency of the batter and the temperature of the pan, both of which may need adjusting.
- If more convenient, pancakes can be made ahead of time. Cool, then stack them, interleaved with greaseproof, and wrap in foil. They can be refrigerated for up to 3 days or frozen for 1 month.
- A pancake pan has a flat bottom and sides that rise straight out of it without curving; these give the pancake a well-defined edge.

FRUIT & ICES

~

Fruit is a colourful and healthy way to end a meal, and this chapter shows how to prepare fruit to achieve a beautiful presentation; to make fruit salads and refreshing iced desserts such as sorbets and ice creams.

PREPARING FRESH FRUIT

PEELING AND TRIMMING FRUIT

Citrus fruit

To peel completely, cut a slice from the top and from the base. Set the fruit base down on a work surface. Using a small sharp knife, cut off the peel lengthways in thick strips. Take the coloured zest and all the white pith (which has a bitter taste). Cut following the curve of the fruit.

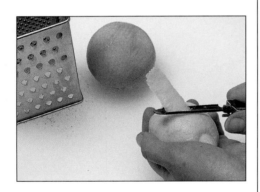

To remove zest, use a vegetable peeler to shave off the zest in wide strips, taking none of the white pith. Use these strips whole or cut them into fine shreds with a sharp knife, according to recipe directions. Or rub the fruit against the fine holes of a metal grater, turning the fruit so you take just the coloured zest and not the white pith. Or use a special tool, called a citrus zester, to take fine threads of zest. (Finely chop the threads as an alternative to grating.)

Kiwi fruit

Follow citrus fruit technique, taking off the peel in thin lengthways strips.

Apples, pears, quinces, mangoes, papayas

Use a small sharp knife or a vegetable peeler. Take off the peel in long strips, as thinly as possible.

Peaches, apricots

Cut a cross in the base. Immerse the fruit in boiling water. Leave for 10–30 seconds (according to ripeness), then drain and immerse in iced water. The skin should slip off easily.

Pineapple

Cut off the leafy crown. Cut a slice from the base and set the pineapple upright. With a sharp knife, cut off the peel lengthways, cutting thickly to remove the brown 'eyes' with it.

Bananas, lychees, avocado

Make a small cut and remove the peel with your fingers.

Passion fruit, pomegranates

Cut in half, or cut a slice off the top. With a spoon, scoop the flesh and seeds into a bowl.

Star fruit (carambola)

Trim off the tough, darkened edges of the five segments.

Rhubarb

Cut off the leaves and discard them (they are poisonous). Peel off any tough skin.

Fresh currants (red, black, white)
Pull through the prongs of a fork to remove the currants from the stalks.

Fresh dates
Squeeze gently at the stalk end to remove the rather tough skin.

CORING AND STONING OR SEEDING FRUIT

Apples, pears, quinces
For whole fruit, use an apple corer to stamp out the whole core from stalk end to base. Alternatively, working up from the base, use a melon baller to cut out the core. Leave the stalk end intact.

For halves, use a melon baller to scoop out the core. Cut out the stalk and base with a small sharp knife.
For quarters, cut out the stalk and core with a serrated knife.

Citrus fruit
With the tip of a pointed knife, nick out pips from slices or segments.

Cherries
Use a cherry stoner for the neatest results.

Peaches, apricots, nectarines, plums
Cut the fruit in half, cutting round the indentation. Twist the halves apart. Lift out the stone, or lever it out with the tip of a sharp knife.

Fresh dates
Cut the fruit lengthways in half and lift out the stone. Or, if the fruit is to be used whole, cut in from the stalk end with a thin-bladed knife to loosen the stone, then remove it.

Mangoes
Cut lengthways on either side of the large flat stone in the centre. Curve the cut slightly to follow the shape of the stone. Also cut the flesh from the two thin ends of the stone.

Papayas, melons
Cut the fruit in half. Scoop out the seeds from the central hollow, then scrape away any fibres.

Pineapple

For spears and wedges, cut out the core neatly with a sharp knife.

For rings, cut out the core with a small pastry cutter.

Grapes

Cut the fruit lengthways in half. Use a small knife to nick out the pips. Alternatively, use the curved end of a sterilized hair grip.

Gooseberries

Use scissors to trim off the stalk and flower ends.

Star fruit (carambola), watermelon

With the tip of a pointed knife, nick out pips from slices.

Strawberries

Use a special huller to remove leafy green top and central core. Or cut these out with a small sharp knife.

Avocado

Cut the fruit in half lengthways. Stick the tip of a sharp knife into the stone and lever it out without damaging the surrounding flesh.

CUTTING FRUIT

Apples, quinces

For rings, remove the core and seeds with an apple corer. Set the fruit on its side and cut across into thick or thin rings, as required.

For slices, cut the fruit in half and remove core and seeds with a melon baller. Set one half cut side down and

cut it across into neat slices, thick or thin according to recipe directions. Or cut the fruit into quarters and remove core and seeds with a knife. Cut lengthways into neat slices.

Pears

For 'fans', cut the fruit in half and remove core and seeds with a melon baller. Set one half cut side down and cut lengthways into thin slices, not cutting all the way through at the stalk end. Gently fan out the slices so they are overlapping each other evenly. Transfer the pear fan to plate or pastry case using a palette knife.

For slices, follow apple technique.

Keeping fresh colour

If exposed to the air for long, the cut flesh of some fruits and vegetables starts to turn brown. Those with a tendency to brown include apples, bananas, peaches and avocado. So if prepared fruit has to wait before being served or cooked, sprinkle the cut surfaces with lemon juice. Or you can immerse hard fruits in water and lemon juice, but do not soak or the fruit may become soggy.

Citrus fruit

For slices, using a serrated knife, cut the fruit across into neat slices.

For segments, hold the peeled fruit in your cupped palm, over a bowl to catch the juice. Working from the side of the fruit to the centre, slide the knife down one side of a separating membrane to free the flesh from it. Then slide the knife down the other side of that segment to free it from the membrane there. Drop the segment into the bowl. Continue cutting out the segments, folding back the membrane like the pages of a book as you work. When all the segments have been cut out, squeeze all the juice from the membrane.

Peaches, nectarines, apricots, plums

For slices, follow apple technique.

Papayas, avocado

For slices, follow apple technique. Or cut the unpeeled fruit into wedges, removing the central seeds or stone. Set each wedge peel side down and slide the knife down the length to cut the flesh away from the peel.
For fans, follow pear technique.

Melon

For slices, follow papaya technique.
For balls, use a melon baller.

Mangoes

Cut the peeled flesh into slices or cubes, according to recipe directions.

Bananas Baked with Rum

Quarter 4 bananas and put in a small baking dish. Sprinkle with a mixture of 2 oz (55 g) melted butter, 3 tablespoons soft light brown sugar, 1–2 tablespoons lemon juice and 6 tablespoons light rum or orange juice. Turn to coat. Bake at 400°F/200°C/ Gas 6 for 20 minutes, basting occasionally. Serve with cream. *Serves 4.*

Pineapple

For spears, cut the peeled fruit lengthways in half and then into quarters. Cut each quarter into spears and cut out the core.
For chunks, cut the peeled fruit into spears. Remove the core. Cut across each spear into chunks.
For rings, cut the peeled fruit across into slices. Stamp out the central core from each slice using a pastry cutter.

Kiwi fruit, star fruit (carambola)

Cut the fruit across into neat slices; discard the ends.

Banana

Cut the fruit across into neat slices. Or cut in half and then lengthways into quarters.

PREPARING MELON

Melons make attractive containers for salads, both sweet and savoury. Small melons can be used for individual servings, while large watermelons will hold salads to serve a crowd and provide a festive centrepiece at the same time!

Special tools, such as melon cutters with V- or U-shaped blades and melon ball scoops, make decorative preparation easier.

1 ◄ **For a plain edge:** Cut the melon in half and scoop out the central seeds. Remove the flesh with a melon baller. Or cut it out with a grapefruit knife or scoop it out with a large spoon. Reserve the flesh for the salad. Continue scraping out the flesh, to leave only a thin layer.

2 ▲ **For a zig-zag edge:** First cut a line around the circumference of the melon to ensure that your finished edge will be level. Using a sharp knife, insert it on the cut line at an angle. Continue making an angled cut about ½–2 in (1.5–5 cm) long, according to the size of the melon. Cut all the way into the centre of the melon. Remove the knife.

3 ▲ Insert the knife at the top of the angled cut and cut back down to the line at a right angle to the first cut, forming a V. Continue cutting V-shapes in this way all round the melon. If available, a special melon cutter with a V-shaped blade will make the job easier.

4 ▲ Lift the melon halves apart. Remove the seeds and scoop out the flesh as above.

Watermelon Basket
Cut a watermelon basket as directed above. Scoop out the flesh with a melon baller and nick out as many of the black pips as you can. Mix the melon balls with balls of charentais and honeydew melon, blueberries and strawberries. Pile the fruit in the watermelon basket for serving.

Citrus garnishes
The technique for preparing melons can also be used for lemons and oranges. These make attractive containers for cold and iced desserts. Another idea: cut a lemon in half with a zig-zag edge, but don't hollow out the halves. Instead, trim the base of each so it will sit flat, then dip the points of the edge in chopped parsley. Serve this instead of plain lemon wedges with fish.

5 ▲ **For a scalloped edge:** You can do this freehand following the technique for cutting a zig-zag edge, but instead cutting curves. However, it is much easier, and the results are better, if you use a special melon cutter with a U-shaped blade.

6 ▲ For a melon basket: Cut a plain, zig-zag or scalloped edge, starting just off centre. Cut round the melon to a point opposite where you started.

7 ▲ Cut up over the top of the melon and down to the point you began. Lift off the freed wedge of melon. Repeat on the other end.

8 ▲ Cut out the flesh from under the 'handle'. Cut the flesh from the 'basket' as shown.

Melon Salad with Herbs

SERVES 4

| 2 charentais melons |
| ½ honeydew melon |
| ½ cucumber |
| 6 oz (170 g) small cherry tomatoes |
| 1½ tablespoons chopped fresh parsley |
| 1 tablespoon snipped fresh chives |
| 1 tablespoon chopped fresh mint |
| FOR THE DRESSING |
| 6 tablespoons vegetable oil |
| 2 tablespoons red wine vinegar |
| 1 teaspoon caster sugar |
| salt and pepper |

1 Cut the charentais in half, with a plain, zig-zag or scalloped edge. Scoop out the seeds and central fibres. Using a melon baller, take small balls of flesh and put them in a bowl. Scrape most of the remaining flesh from the melon halves. Set the melon shells aside.

2 Remove seeds and fibres from the honeydew melon. Scoop out the flesh in small balls and add to the charentais balls.

3 ▲ Use the melon baller to make balls of cucumber, or cut into cubes.

4 Add the cucumber to the melon balls with the cherry tomatoes.

5 For the dressing, combine the ingredients in a screwtop jar and shake well. Add the dressing to the bowl and toss together. Cover and refrigerate the salad for 2–3 hours.

6 Just before serving, stir in the herbs. Divide the salad among the melon shells, with all the juice.

PREPARING FRESH PINEAPPLE

Pineapple can be prepared in many decorative ways, apart from rings, spears and cubes.

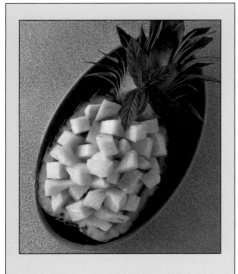

Tipsy Pineapple Boat
Cut 2 small to medium-sized pineapples in half and scoop out the flesh. Cut the pineapple flesh into neat, small pieces. Put them back in the pineapple halves. Sprinkle each half with 1–2 table-spoons rum, kirsch, apricot brandy or Grand Marnier. If liked, sprinkle with a little sugar to taste. Toss the fruit to mix the liquor and sugar evenly. Cover tightly and chill for 20–30 minutes before serving. *Serves 4.*

1 ▲ For a pineapple boat: Trim off any browned ends from the green leaves of the crown. Trim the stalk end if necessary. With a long sharp knife, cut the pineapple lengthways in half, through the crown.

2 ▲ Cut a thin slice from the base of each half so it has a flat surface and will not rock.

3 ▲ With a small sharp knife, cut straight across the top and bottom of the central core in each half. Then cut lengthways at a slant on either side of the core. This will cut out the core in a V-shape.

4 ▲ With a curved serrated grapefruit knife, cut out the flesh from each half. The boats are now ready for filling with a salad, a dessert, or with ice cream, fruit ice or sorbet.

5 ▲ For pineapple wedges: Trim the crown and base as above. Cut the fruit lengthways in half, through the crown, and then into quarters.

6 ▲ Cut the central core from each quarter. Slide the knife under the flesh to loosen it from the peel, but leave it in place.

7 ▲ Cut across the flesh on each wedge. Pull out the slices slightly in alternate directions. If desired, sprinkle the fruit lightly with sugar before serving.

MAKING SORBETS AND FRUIT ICES

Sorbets and fruit ices are most refreshing desserts. A fruit ice is made by freezing a sweetened fruit purée, whereas a sorbet is made from fruit juice or purée mixed with a sugar syrup. In addition, there are sorbets based on wine or liqueur. The Italian 'granita' uses the same mixture as a sorbet, but it is stirred during freezing to give it its characteristic coarse texture. A sherbet normally contains milk or cream.

Strawberry Ice
Purée 1 lb 2 oz (500 g) strawberries with 3½ oz (100 g) caster sugar and 4 fl oz (120 ml) orange juice. Be sure the sugar has dissolved completely. Add 1 tablespoon lemon juice. Taste the mixture and add more sugar or orange or lemon juice if required. (The mixture should be highly flavoured.) Chill well, then transfer to an ice cream machine and freeze until firm. *Makes about 1 pint (600 ml).*

Variations
• Use raspberries or blackberries instead of strawberries.
• Use 1½ lb (700 g) peeled and sliced peaches or nectarines instead of strawberries.
• Add 1–2 tablespoons of fruit liqueur (to match the fruit used).

1 ▲ For a fruit ice: Prepare the fruit, removing peel, stones, hulls, stalks, etc. Purée the fruit with sugar and liquid in a blender or food processor until very smooth. Be sure that the sugar has dissolved completely.

3 ▲ For a sorbet: If using citrus fruit, peel off strips of zest. Squeeze the juice from the fruit. Alternatively, purée fruit in a blender or food processor (first cooking if necessary).

5 ▲ Stir in the fruit juice or purée. Strain the mixture into a bowl, if necessary, and chill well. Then transfer the mixture to an ice cream machine and freeze following the manufacturer's instructions.

2 ▲ Add additional flavourings as directed in the recipe (alcohol, herbs, for example). If using berries with seeds (raspberries, blackberries, etc), press the purée through a fine-mesh nylon sieve. Chill the purée well. Then transfer to an ice cream machine and freeze following the manufacturer's instructions.

4 ▲ Put the strips of zest (or other flavouring items such as vanilla pod, spices) in a saucepan with sugar and water and bring to the boil, stirring to dissolve the sugar. Leave to cool.

Still-freezing fruit ice
If you don't have an ice cream machine, you can 'still-freeze' the fruit ice or sorbet in the freezer. Pour it into a metal tin or tray, cover and freeze until set round the edge. Turn it into a bowl and break it into small pieces. Beat with an electric mixer or in a food processor until slushy. Return to the metal tin and freeze again until set round the edge. Repeat the beating once or twice more, then freeze until firm.

MAKING A BERRY SAUCE

A smooth, uncooked berry sauce, called a 'coulis' in French, has a refreshing flavour and beautiful colour. According to how much sugar you add, a berry sauce can be a sweet complement or tart contrast to a cake, pastry, ice cream or fruit dessert.

You can use fresh or frozen berries for the sauce. If using frozen berries, partially thaw them and drain on paper towels before puréeing.

MAKES ABOUT 8 FL OZ (240 ML)

1 lb (450 g) berries (raspberries, strawberries, blackberries, etc)

1–2 oz (30–55 g) icing sugar, sifted

squeeze of lemon juice (optional)

1–2 tablespoons kirsch or fruit liqueur (optional)

1 ▲ Hull the berries if necessary. Put them in a bowl of cold water and swirl them round briefly. Scoop out and spread on paper towels. Pat dry. Purée the berries in a blender or food processor. Turn the machine on and off a few times and scrape down the bowl to be sure all the berries are evenly puréed.

2 ▲ For raspberries, blackberries and other berries with small seeds, press the purée through a fine-mesh nylon sieve. Add icing sugar to taste, plus a little lemon juice and/or liqueur, if using (for example, raspberry liqueur – framboise – for a raspberry sauce). Stir well to dissolve the sugar completely.

Iced Macaroon Cream with Raspberry Sauce

SERVES 6–8

1¼ pints (750 ml) whipping cream

4 tablespoons brandy or orange juice

2 tablespoons caster sugar

12 crisp almond macaroons (about 4 oz/ 115 g), coarsely crushed

raspberries, to decorate

8 fl oz (240 ml) raspberry sauce, to serve

2 Add the brandy or juice and sugar. Continue whipping until the cream will hold stiff peaks.

3 ▼ Add the macaroons and fold evenly into the cream.

4 Spoon into 6–8 ramekins, or a 2 pint (1.5 litre) smooth-sided mould. Press in evenly to be sure there are no air pockets. Smooth the surface. Cover and freeze until firm. (Do not freeze longer than 1 day.)

5 ▼ To serve, dip the moulds in hot water for 5–10 seconds, then invert on to a serving plate. Lift off the moulds. Refrigerate the desserts for 15–20 minutes to soften slightly.

1 ▲ Put the cream in a large bowl, preferably chilled, and whip until it starts to thicken.

~ VARIATION ~

Use coarsely broken meringue nests instead of macaroons. Use almond liqueur instead of brandy or juice.

6 Decorate with raspberries and serve with the sauce.

BREADS & CAKES

~

*There is nothing quite so satisfying as the aroma of freshly
baked bread. Even if you're a beginner, you'll find the
methods for teabreads and yeast breads, and the cake-making
techniques easy to follow.*

MAKING TEABREADS AND MUFFINS

These sorts of bread are very quick and easy to make. The raising agent reacts quickly with moisture and heat to make the breads and muffins rise, without the need for a rising (or proving) period before baking.

The raising agent is usually bicarbonate of soda or baking powder, which is a mixture of bicarbonate of soda and an acid salt such as cream of tartar. Many recipes use self-raising flour which conveniently includes a raising agent. Remember that the raising agent will start to work as soon as it comes into contact with liquid, so don't mix the dry and liquid ingredients until just before you are ready to fill the tin or tins and bake.

1 ▲ **For muffins:** Combine the dry ingredients in a bowl. It is a good idea to sift the flour with the raising agent, salt and any spices to mix them evenly. Add the liquid ingredients and stir just until the dry ingredients are moistened; the mixture will not be smooth. Do not overmix attempting to remove all the lumps. If you do, the muffins will be tough and will have air holes in them.

2 ▲ Divide the mixture evenly among the greased muffin tins or deep bun tins lined with paper cases, filling them about two-thirds full. Bake until golden brown and a wooden skewer inserted in the centre comes out clean. To prevent soggy bottoms, remove the muffins immediately from the tins to a wire rack. Cool, and serve warm or at room temperature.

Crunchy Muesli Muffins
Make the mixture from 5 oz (145 g) plain flour, 2½ teaspoons baking powder, 2 tablespoons caster sugar, 8 fl oz (240 ml) milk, 2 oz (55 g) melted butter or corn oil, and 1 egg, adding 7 oz (200 g) toasted oat cereal with raisins to the dry ingredients. Pour into muffin tins or deep bun tins. Bake in a 200°C/400°F/Gas 6 oven for 20 minutes or until golden brown. *Makes 10.*

3 ▲ **For fruit and/or nut teabreads:** Method 1: Stir together all the liquid ingredients. Add the dry ingredients and beat just until smoothly blended. Method 2: Beat the butter with the sugar until the mixture is light and fluffy. Beat in the eggs followed by the other liquid ingredients. Stir in the dry ingredients. Pour the mixture into a prepared tin (typically a loaf tin). Bake until a wooden skewer inserted in the centre comes out clean. If the bread is browning too quickly, cover the top with foil.

4 ▲ Cool in the tin for 5 minutes, then turn out on to a wire rack to cool completely. A lengthways crack on the surface is characteristic of teabreads. For easier slicing, wrap the bread in greaseproof paper and overwrap in foil, then store overnight at room temperature.

Banana Bread

MAKES 1 LOAF

7 oz (200 g) plain flour

2¼ teaspoons baking powder

½ teaspoon salt

¾ teaspoon ground cinnamon
   (optional)

4 tablespoons wheat germ

2½ oz (75 g) butter or margarine, at
   room temperature

4 oz (115 g) caster sugar

¾ teaspoon grated lemon zest

3 ripe bananas, mashed

2 eggs, beaten to mix

1 Preheat a 350°F/180°C/Gas 4 oven. Grease and flour an 8½ × 4½ in (21 × 11 cm) loaf tin.

2 ▲ Sift the flour, baking powder, salt and cinnamon, if using, into a bowl. Stir in the wheat germ.

3 ▲ In another bowl, combine the butter or margarine with the sugar and lemon zest. Beat until the mixture is light and fluffy.

4 ▲ Add the mashed bananas and eggs and mix well.

5 Add the dry ingredients and blend quickly and evenly.

~ VARIATION ~

For Banana Walnut Bread, add 2–3 oz (55–85 g) finely chopped walnuts with the dry ingredients.

6 ▼ Spoon into the prepared loaf tin. Bake for 50–60 minutes or until a wooden skewer inserted in the centre comes out clean.

7 Cool in the pan for about 5 minutes, then turn out on to a wire rack to cool completely.

MAKING YEAST DOUGH

Making bread is a very enjoyable and satisfying culinary experience – with no other preparation do you have such 'hands-on' contact. And from the kneading through to the shaping of the risen (or proven) dough, you are working with a living organism, yeast, not a chemical raising agent. You can use either fresh yeast or dried yeast, which is available in an easy-blend variety too.

Everyday White Bread
Sift 1½ lb (700 g) strong plain flour into a large bowl with 1½ teaspoons salt and 1 tablespoon caster sugar. Stir in 2 teaspoons easy-blend dried yeast. Make a well in the centre and add ¾ pint (450 ml) mixed warm water and milk and 1 oz (30 g) melted and cooled butter. Mix to a soft dough, adding more flour or liquid if necessary, then knead until smooth and elastic. Leave to rise until doubled in bulk. Knock back the dough to deflate. Divide it in half and shape each piece into a loaf, tucking the ends under. Put in 2 greased 8½ × 4½ in (21 × 11 cm) loaf tins. Leave in a warm place to rise for 30–45 minutes. Glaze the tops of the loaves with 1 egg beaten with 1 tablespoon milk. Bake in a 450°F/230°C/Gas 8 oven for 30–35 minutes. *Makes 2 loaves.*

1 ▲ If using ordinary dried yeast, put it in a small bowl, add some of the warm liquid (105–110°F/40–43°C) called for in the recipe and whisk with a fork until dissolved. Add a little sugar if the recipe specifies.

3 ▲ Using your fingers or a spoon, gradually draw the flour into the liquids. Mix until all the flour is incorporated and the dough pulls away from the sides of the bowl. If the dough feels too soft and wet, work in a little more flour. If it doesn't come together, add a little more liquid.

5 ▲ Shape the dough into a ball. Put it in a lightly greased bowl and turn the dough to grease all over. Cover the bowl with a towel or cling film. Set it aside in a warm, draught-free place (about 80°F/27°C).

2 ▲ Sift the flour into a large warm bowl (with other dry ingredients such as salt). Make a well in the centre and add the yeast mixture plus any other liquid ingredients.

4 ▲ Turn the dough on to a lightly floured surface. Fold the dough over on to itself towards you and then press it down away from you with the heels of your hands. Rotate the dough slightly and fold and press it again. Knead until the dough looks satiny and feels elastic, about 10 minutes.

6 ▲ Leave to rise until about doubled in bulk, 1–1½ hours. To test if it is sufficiently risen, press a finger about 1 in (2.5 cm) into the dough and withdraw it quickly; the indentation should remain.

7 ▲ Gently punch the centre of the dough with your fist to deflate it and fold the edges to the centre. Turn the dough on to a lightly floured surface and knead it again for 2–3 minutes. If instructed, shape the dough into a ball again and rise a second time.

8 ▲ Shape the dough into loaves, rolls or other shapes as instructed. Put into prepared tins or on to baking sheets. Cover and leave to rise in a warm place for ¾–1 hour. If the recipe instructs, glaze the loaves or rolls.

9 ◀ Bake in the centre of a heated oven until well risen and golden brown. To test, tip the loaf out of the tin and tap the base with your knuckle. If it sounds hollow, like a drum, it is fully cooked. Immediately transfer to a wire rack for cooling.

SHAPING ROLLS

A basket of freshly baked bread rolls, in decorative shapes, is a delightful accompaniment for soups or salads. After shaping, arrange the rolls on a baking sheet, leaving space around each roll for spreading, and leave to rise for 30 minutes before baking.

Working with yeast

Easy-blend (or fast-action) is the most readily available dried yeast. Unlike ordinary dried yeast, there is no need to mix it with liquid. Just combine it with the flour and other dry ingredients and then add the warm liquids.

If using fresh yeast, allow ½ oz (15 g) to each 1 tablespoon dried. Crumble it into a small bowl, add warm liquid and mash with a fork until blended.

If you are in any doubt about the freshness of ordinary dried or fresh yeast, set the mixture aside in a warm place; after 10 minutes or so it should be foamy. If it isn't, discard it.

1 ▲ For Parker House rolls: Roll out the risen dough to ¼ in (5 mm) thickness and cut out 2½–3 in (6–7 cm) rounds using a floured cutter. Brush the rounds with melted butter. Fold them in half, slightly off-centre so the top overlaps the bottom. Press the folded edge firmly. Arrange the rolls on a greased baking sheet.

2 ▲ For crescent rolls: Roll out the risen dough to a large round ¼ in (5 mm) thick. Brush with melted butter. With a sharp knife, cut into wedges that are 2½–3 in (6–7 cm) at their wide end. Roll up each wedge, from the wide end. Set the rolls on a greased baking sheet, placing the points underneath.

3 ◀ For bowknot rolls: Divide the risen dough into pieces. Roll each with your palms on a lightly floured surface to make ropes that are about ½ in (1.5 cm) thick. Divide the ropes into 9 in (27 cm) lengths. Tie each rope loosely into a knot, tucking the ends under. Arrange the rolls on a greased baking sheet.

MAKING CAKES BY THE CREAMING METHOD

The Victoria sandwich, with its tender crumb and rich, moist flavour, is always popular. It is delicious enough to be served plain, with just a dusting of sugar, or it can be filled and iced.

To make cakes by the creaming method, the fat and sugar are 'creamed' – or beaten – together before the eggs and dry ingredients are added. The fat (usually butter or margarine) should be soft enough to be beaten, so if necessary remove it from the refrigerator and leave it at room temperature for at least 30 minutes. For best results, the eggs should be at room temperature.

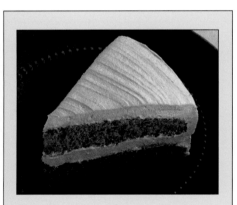

Mocha Victoria Sponge
Make the mixture using 6 oz (170 g) each butter or margarine, caster sugar and self-raising flour and 3 eggs. Divide between two bowls. To one add 1 tablespoon strong black coffee; to the other add 1 tablespoon cocoa powder mixed to a paste with 1–2 tablespoons boiling water. Place alternate spoonfuls of each flavour, side by side, in 2 greased and bottom-lined 7 in (18 cm) round sandwich tins. Lightly smooth the top. Bake at 350°F/180°C/ Gas 4 for 25–30 minutes. Turn out on to a wire rack and cool. Sandwich the cakes together with coffee buttercream. Cover the top of the cake, or the top and sides, with buttercream.

1 ▲ Sift the flour with the salt, raising agent(s) and any other dry ingredients, such as spices or cocoa powder. Set aside.

3 ▲ Add the sugar to the creamed fat gradually. With the mixer at medium-high speed, beat it into the fat until the mixture is pale and very fluffy. The sugar should be completely incorporated. This will take 4–5 minutes. During this process, air will be beaten into the mixture, which will help the cake to rise.

5 ▲ Add the dry ingredients to the mixture, beating at low speed just until smoothly combined. Or fold in with a large metal spoon.

2 ▲ Put the fat in a large, deep bowl and beat with an electric mixer at medium speed, or a wooden spoon, until the texture is soft and pliable.

4 ▲ Add the eggs or egg yolks, one at a time, beating well after each addition (about 45 seconds). Scrape the bowl often so all the ingredients are evenly combined. When adding the eggs, the mixture may begin to curdle, especially if the eggs are cold. If this happens, add 1 tablespoon of the measured flour.

6 ▲ If the recipe calls for any liquid, add it in small portions alternately with portions of the dry ingredients.

7 ▲ If the recipe specifies, whisk egg whites separately until frothy, add sugar and continue whisking until stiff peaks form. Fold into the mixture.

8 ▲ Pour the mixture into a cake tin or tins, prepared according to the recipe, and bake as specified.

9 ▲ To test creamed-method cakes, insert a metal skewer or wooden cocktail stick into the centre; it should come out clean.

MAKING AMERICAN FROSTING

This fluffy white frosting has an attractive gloss and a texture like meringue. It is a delicious filling and icing for sanwich cakes.

MAKES ENOUGH TO FILL AND ICE A 9 IN (23 CM) SANDWICH CAKE

10 oz (300 g) sugar
¼ teaspoon cream of tartar
2 egg whites
4 tablespoons cold water
1 tablespoon liquid glucose
2 teaspoons vanilla essence

1 ▲ Combine the sugar, cream of tartar, egg whites, water and glucose in a large heatproof bowl or the top of a double saucepan. Stir just to mix.

2 ▲ Set the bowl over a saucepan of boiling water. The base of the bowl should not touch the water.

Frosting variations

For *Orange Frosting*: Use orange juice instead of water and add 1 teaspoon grated orange zest. Reduce the vanilla to ½ teaspoon.

For *Lemon Frosting*: Use 2 tablespoons each lemon juice and water and add ½ teaspoon grated lemon zest. Reduce the vanilla to ½ teaspoon.

3 ▲ Beat with a hand-held electric mixer at high speed for about 7 minutes or until the frosting is thick and white and will form stiff peaks.

4 ▲ Remove from the heat. Add the vanilla and continue beating for about 3 minutes or until the frosting has cooled slightly. Use immediately.

MAKING CAKES BY THE ALL-IN-ONE METHOD

Many cakes are made by an easy all-in-one method where all the ingredients are combined in a bowl and beaten thoroughly. The mixture can also be made in a food processor, but take care not to over-process. A refinement on the all-in-one method is to separate the eggs and make the mixture with the yolks. The whites are whisked separately and then folded in.

1 ▲ Sift the dry ingredients (flour, salt, raising agent, spices and so on) into a bowl.

2 ▲ Add the liquid ingredients (eggs, melted or soft fat, milk, fruit juices and so on) and beat until smooth, with an electric mixer for speed. Pour into the prepared tins and bake as specified in the recipe.

MAKING SIMPLE BUTTERCREAM

Quick to make and easy to spread, buttercream is ideal for all kinds of cakes, from simple ones to gâteaux. The basic buttercream can be varied with many other flavours, and it can be tinted with food colouring, too.

MAKES ENOUGH TO COVER THE TOP AND SIDE OF A 7–8 IN (17–20 CM) CAKE

4 oz (115 g) butter, preferably unsalted, at room temperature

8 oz (225 g) icing sugar, sifted

1 teaspoon vanilla essence

about 2 teaspoons milk

1 ▲ Put the butter in a deep mixing bowl and beat it with an electric mixer at medium speed, or a wooden spoon, until it is soft and pliable.

2 ▲ Gradually add the icing sugar and beat at medium-high speed. Continue beating until the mixture is pale and fluffy.

3 ▲ Add the vanilla essence and 1 tablespoon milk. Beat until smooth and of a spreading consistency. If it is too thick, beat in more milk. If too thin, beat in more sugar.

Buttercream variations

● For *Orange or Lemon Buttercream*, grate the zest from 1 small orange or ½ lemon; squeeze the juice. Beat in the zest with the sugar; use the juice instead of the vanilla and milk.

● For *Chocolate Buttercream*, add 4 tablespoons cocoa powder, beating it in with the sugar. Increase the milk to 3–4 tablespoons.

● For *Mocha Buttercream*: Warm the milk and dissolve 1 teaspoon instant coffee powder in it; cool and use to make chocolate buttercream, adding more milk if needed.

● For *Coffee Buttercream*, warm the milk and dissolve 1 tablespoon of instant coffee powder in it; cool before adding to the buttercream.

Chocolate Fairy Cakes

MAKES 24

4 oz (115 g) good-quality plain
 chocolate, cut into small pieces

1 tablespoon water

10 oz (300 g) plain flour

1 teaspoon baking powder

½ teaspoon bicarbonate of soda

pinch of salt

10 oz (300 g) caster sugar

6 oz (170 g) butter or margarine, at room
 temperature

¼ pint (150 ml) milk

1 teaspoon vanilla essence

3 eggs

1 recipe quantity buttercream, flavoured
 to taste

1 Preheat a 350°F/180°C/Gas 4 oven.
Grease and flour 24 deep bun tins,
about 2¾ in (6.5 cm) in diameter, or
use paper cases in the tins.

2 ▲ Put the chocolate and water in a
bowl set over a pan of almost
simmering water. Heat until melted
and smooth, stirring. Remove from
the heat and leave to cool.

3 Sift the flour, baking powder,
bicarbonate of soda, salt and sugar
into a large bowl. Add the chocolate
mixture, butter, milk and vanilla
essence.

4 ▲ With an electric mixer on
medium-low speed, beat until
smoothly blended. Increase the speed
to high and beat for 2 minutes. Add
the eggs and beat for 2 minutes.

5 Divide the mixture evenly among
the prepared bun tins.

6 Bake for 20–25 minutes or until
a skewer inserted into the centre of a
cake comes out clean. Cool in the tins
for 10 minutes, then turn out to cool
completely on a wire rack.

7 ▼ Ice the top of each cake with
buttercream, swirling it into a peak in
the centre.

PREPARING CAKE TINS

Instructions vary from recipe to recipe for preparing cake tins. Some are simply greased, some are greased and floured, some are lined with baking parchment or greased greaseproof paper. The preparation required depends on the type of cake mixture and the length of the baking time. Proper preparation aids turning out.

Flavourful coatings
Some cake recipes specify that the greased tin be coated with sugar, cocoa powder or ground nuts. Follow the method for flouring.

1 ▲ To grease a tin: Use butter, margarine, or a mild or flavourless oil. If using butter or margarine, hold a small piece in a paper towel (or use your fingers), and rub it all over the bottom and up the side of the tin to make a thin, even coating. If using oil, brush it on with a pastry brush.

2 ▲ To flour a tin: Put a small scoopful of flour in the centre of the greased tin. Tip and rotate the tin so that the flour spreads and coats all over the bottom and up the side. Turn the tin over and shake out excess flour, tapping the base of the tin to dislodge any pockets of flour.

3 ▲ To line the bottom of a tin: Set the tin on the sheet of paper and draw round the base. Cut out this circle, square or rectangle, cutting just inside the drawn line. Press the paper smoothly on to the bottom of the tin.

4 ▲ To line the sides of a tin (for rich mixtures and fruit cakes): Cut a strip of paper long enough to wrap round the outside of the tin and overlap by 1½ in (4 cm). The strip should be wide enough to extend 1 in (2.5 cm) above the rim of the tin.

5 ▲ Fold the strip lengthways at the 1 in (2.5 cm) point and crease firmly. With scissors, snip at regular intervals along the 1 in (2.5 cm) fold, from the edge to the crease. Line the side of the tin, with the snipped part of the strip on the bottom.

6 ▲ For square and rectangular cake tins, fold the paper and crease it with your fingernail to fit snugly into the corners of the tin. Then press the bottom paper lining into place.

7 ▲ If the recipe specifies, grease the paper before you put it in the tin. If the tin is to be floured, do this after the paper is in place.

8 ▲ To line bun and muffin tins: Use paper liners of the required size. Or grease and flour the tins.

9 ▲ **To line a Swiss roll tin:** Cut a rectangle of paper 2 in (5 cm) larger all round than the tin. Grease the bottom of the tin lightly to prevent the paper from slipping.

10 ▲ Lay the paper evenly in the tin. With a table knife, press the paper into the angle all round the bottom of the tin, creasing the paper firmly but not cutting it.

11 ▲ With scissors, snip the paper in the corners, from top to bottom, so it will fit neatly into them. Grease the paper according to recipe instructions, unless using baking parchment.

USING SEPARATED EGGS FOR A WHISKED SPONGE

This version of whisked sponge is easier to make than the classic one that uses whole eggs, but the results are no less light and delicious. There is no need to set the bowl over a pan of simmering water for whisking, although if you are using a balloon whisk rather than an electric mixer or rotary beater you may want to do so to speed up the thickening of the egg yolk and sugar mixture and to increase its volume. Bowls and beaters used with egg whites must be scrupulously clean.

1 ▲ Separate the eggs, taking care that there is no trace of yolk with the whites. Put the yolks and whites in separate large bowls.

2 ▲ Add most of the sugar to the yolks. With a hand-held or table-top electric mixer, whisk at medium-high speed until the mixture is very thick and pale. Lift out the beaters: the mixture on the beaters should trail back on to the surface of the remaining mixture in the bowl to make a ribbon that holds its shape.

3 ▲ Whisk the egg whites until they form soft peaks (if not using a copper bowl, add a pinch of cream of tartar once the whites are frothy). Add the remaining sugar and continue whisking until the whites will form stiff peaks.

4 ▲ With a rubber spatula, fold the sifted flour into the egg yolk mixture, then fold in the whisked egg whites. Fold gently but thoroughly. Pour the mixture into the prepared tin and bake as instructed.

A Genoese sponge
This whisked sponge, made with whole or separated eggs, is more rich and trickier to make, as melted butter is folded in just before pouring into the tin.

MAKING A CLASSIC WHISKED SPONGE

The classic whisked sponge contains no fat and no raising agents – just eggs, sugar and flour. The light, airy texture of the finished cake depends on the large quantity of air beaten into the mixture.

Sometimes the eggs are separated for a whisked sponge and sometimes the cake is enriched with butter. American angel food cake uses egg whites only.

A whisked sponge can be simply dusted with icing or caster sugar, filled with sweetened whipped cream, a fruit jam or fresh fruit, or used to make a Swiss roll.

If you use a table-top electric mixer to beat the eggs and sugar, or if using separated eggs, there is no need to set the bowl over a pan of simmering water.

Whisked Sponge
Make the mixture using 4 whole eggs, 5 oz (145 g) caster sugar and 4 oz (115 g) plain flour. Pour into a greased, bottom-lined and floured 9 in (23 cm) round cake tin. Bake in a 350°F/180°C/Gas 4 oven for 25–30 minutes. Cool in the tin for 10 minutes, then turn out on to a wire rack and cool completely. Before serving, peel off the lining paper. Dust the top lightly with sifted icing sugar.

1 ▲ In a heatproof bowl, combine the eggs (at room temperature) and sugar. Set the bowl over a saucepan of simmering water; the base of the bowl should not touch the water.

3 ▲ Lift out the beaters; the mixture on the beaters should trail back on to the surface of the remaining mixture in the bowl to make a ribbon that holds its shape.

5 ▲ Sift the flour and fold it into the mixture, cutting in to the bottom of the bowl with a rubber spatula or large metal spoon and turning the mixture over, working gently yet thoroughly to retain the volume of the whisked egg and sugar mixture.

2 ▲ Beat with a hand-held electric mixer at medium-high speed, or a rotary beater or whisk, until the mixture is very thick and pale – about 10 minutes.

4 ▲ Remove the bowl from over the pan of water and continue beating for 2–3 minutes or until the mixture is cool.

6 ▲ Pour the mixture into the prepared tin or tins and bake as directed in the recipe. To test a whisked sponge, press the centre lightly with your fingertip: the cake should spring back.

MAKING A SWISS ROLL

A rolled sponge reveals an attractive spiral of filling when it is sliced. The filling may be sweetened whipped cream, ice cream, fruit jam or buttercream. The whisked sponge mixture can be made using whole or separated eggs, as preferred.

Line the tin with greaseproof paper or baking parchment. Lightly grease the paper and dust with a little flour, shaking off any excess.

Chocolate Ice Cream Roll
Make the sponge mixture using 4 eggs, separated, 4 oz (115 g) caster sugar and 4 oz (115 g) plain flour sifted with 3 tablespoons cocoa powder. Pour into a prepared 15 10 in (37.5 × 25 cm) Swiss roll tin. Bake in a 375°F/190°C/Gas 5 oven for about 15 minutes. Turn out, roll up and cool. When cold, unroll the cake and spread with 1 pint (600 ml) softened vanilla or chocolate ice cream. Roll up the cake again, wrap in foil and freeze until firm. About 30 minutes before serving, transfer the cake to the refrigerator. Sprinkle the cake with caster or icing sugar before serving. If desired, serve with warm bittersweet chocolate sauce. *Serves 8.*

1 ▲ Pour the mixture into the prepared tin and spread it evenly into the corners with a palette knife. Bake as specified in the recipe.

3 ▲ Carefully peel off the lining paper from the cake. If necessary, trim off any crisp edges from the side of the cake.

5 ▲ Remove the towel and unroll the cake. Lift off the paper. Spread the chosen filling over the cake.

2 ▲ Spread a tea towel flat and lay a sheet of baking parchment on top. Sprinkle the paper evenly, as specified, with caster or icing sugar, cocoa or a sugar and spice mixture. Invert the cake on to the paper.

4 ▲ Carefully roll up the cake, with the paper inside, starting from a short side. Wrap the towel round the cake roll and leave to cool on a wire rack.

6 ▲ Roll up the cake again, using the paper to help move it forward. Sprinkle with sugar or ice the cake, as the recipe specifies.

PASTRY

~

Making light, crisp pastry needn't be difficult, and the step-by-step pictures help achieve a good result every time. Various pastries are described, with techniques for handling pastry and how to decorate the finished product.

MAKING SHORTCRUST PASTRY

A meltingly short, crumbly pastry sets off any filling to perfection, whether sweet or savoury. The pastry dough can be made with half butter or margarine and half white vegetable fat or with all one kind of fat.

FOR A 9 IN (23 CM) PASTRY CASE

8 oz (225 g) plain flour
¼ teaspoon salt
4 oz (115 g) fat, chilled and diced
3–4 tablespoons iced water

1 ▲ Sift the flour and salt into a bowl. Add the fat. Rub it into the flour with your fingertips until the mixture is crumb-like.

2 ▲ Sprinkle 3 tablespoons water over the mixture. With a fork, toss gently to mix and moisten it.

Pastry making tips

• It helps if the fat is cold and firm, particularly if making the dough in a food processor. Cold fat has less chance of warming and softening too much when it is being rubbed into the flour, resulting in an oily pastry. Use block margarine rather than the soft tub-type.

• When rubbing the fat into the flour, if it begins to soften and feel oily, put the bowl in the refrigerator to chill for 20–30 minutes. Then continue making the dough.

• Liquids used should be ice-cold so that they will not soften or melt the fat.

• Take care when adding the water: start with the smaller amount (added all at once, not in a dribble), and add more only if the mixture will not come together into a dough. Too much water will result in tough pastry.

• When gathering the mixture together into a ball of dough, handle it as little as possible: overworked pastry will be tough.

• To avoid shrinkage, refrigerate the pastry dough before rolling out and baking. This 'resting time' will allow any elasticity developed during mixing to relax.

4 ▲ Press the dough into a ball. If it is too dry to form a dough, add the remaining water.

7 ▲ **To make pastry in a food processor:** Combine the flour, salt and cubed fat in the work bowl. Process, turning the machine on and off, just until the mixture is crumbly. Add the iced water and process again briefly – just until the dough starts to pull away from the sides of the bowl. It should still look crumbly. Remove the dough from the processor and gather it into a ball. Wrap and refrigerate.

5 ▲ Wrap the ball of dough with cling film or greaseproof paper and refrigerate it for at least 30 minutes.

Shortcrust pastry variations

• For *Nut Shortcrust:* Add 1 oz (30 g) finely chopped walnuts or pecan nuts to the flour mixture.

• For *Rich Shortcrust:* Use 8 oz (225 g) flour and 6 oz (170 g) fat (preferably all butter), plus 1 tablespoon caster sugar if making a sweet pie. Bind with 1 egg yolk and 2–3 tablespoons water.

• For a *Two-crust Pie,* increase the proportions for these pastries by 50%, thus the amounts needed for basic shortcrust pastry are: 12 oz (340 g) flour, ½ teaspoon salt, 6 oz (170 g) fat, 5–6 tablespoons water. For Nut Shortcrust, as above with 2 oz (55 g) nuts. For Rich Shortcrust, as above but using 9 oz (260 g) fat, 4–5 tablespoons water and 1 egg yolk.

MAKING FRENCH FLAN PASTRY

The pastry for tarts, flans and quiches is made with butter or margarine, giving a rich and crumbly result. The more fat used, the richer the pastry will be – almost like a biscuit dough – and the harder to roll out. If you have difficulty rolling it, you can press it into the tin instead, or roll it out between sheets of cling film. Flan pastry, like shortcrust, can be made by hand or in a food processor. Tips for making, handling and using shortcrust pastry apply equally to French flan pastry.

FOR A 9 IN (23 CM) FLAN CASE

7 oz (200 g) plain flour
½ teaspoon salt
4 oz (115 g) butter or margarine, chilled
1 egg yolk
¼ teaspoon lemon juice
2–3 tablespoons iced water

1 ▲ Sift the flour and salt into a bowl. Add the butter or margarine. Rub into the flour until the mixture resembles fine crumbs.

2 ▲ In a small bowl, mix the egg yolk, lemon juice and 2 tablespoons water. Add to the flour mixture. With a fork, toss gently to mix and moisten.

3 ▲ Press the dough into a rough ball. If it is too dry to come together, add the remaining water. Turn on to the work surface or a pastry board.

4 ▲ With the heel of your hand, push small portions of dough away from you, smearing them on the surface.

Flan pastry variations
• For *Sweet Flan Pastry:* Reduce the amount of salt to ¼ teaspoon; add 1 tablespoon caster sugar with the flour.
• For *Rich Flan Pastry:* Use 7 oz (200 g) flour, ½ teaspoon salt, 5 oz (145 g) butter, 2 egg yolks, and 1–2 tablespoons water.
• For *Rich Sweet Flan Pastry:* Make rich flan pastry, adding 3 tablespoons caster sugar with the flour and, if liked, ½ teaspoon vanilla essence with the egg yolks.

5 ▲ Continue mixing the dough in this way until it feels pliable and can be peeled easily off the surface.

6 ▲ Press the dough into a smooth ball. Wrap in cling film and chill for at least 30 minutes.

ROLLING OUT AND LINING A TIN

A neat pastry case that doesn't distort or shrink in baking is the desired result. The key to success is handling the dough gently. Use the method here for lining a round pie or tart tin that is about 2 in (5 cm) deep.

Remove the chilled dough from the refrigerator and allow it to soften slightly at room temperature. Unwrap and put it on a lightly floured surface. Flatten the dough into a neat, round disc. Lightly flour the rolling pin.

Rolling out and lining tips
- Reflour the surface and rolling pin if the dough starts to stick.
- Should the dough tear, patch with a piece of moistened dough.
- When rolling out and lining the pie or tart tin, do not stretch the dough. It will only shrink back during baking, spoiling the shape of the pastry case.
- Once or twice during rolling out, gently push in the edges of the dough with your cupped palms, to keep the circular shape.
- A pastry scraper will help lift the dough from the work surface, to wrap it around the rolling pin.
- Tins made from heat-resistant glass or dull-finish metal such as heavyweight aluminium will give a crisp crust.
- When finishing the edge, be sure to hook the dough over the rim all the way round or to press the dough firmly to the rim. This will prevent the dough pulling away should it start to shrink.
- If covering a pie dish, roll the dough to a round or oval 2 in (5 cm) larger than the dish. Cut a 1 in (2.5 cm) strip from the outside and lay this on the moistened rim of the dish. Brush the strip with water and lay the sheet of dough on top. Press edges to seal, then trim even with the rim. Knock up the edge with a knife.

1 ▲ Using even pressure, start rolling out the dough, working from the centre to the edge each time and easing the pressure slightly as you reach the edge.

2 ▲ Lift up the dough and give it a quarter turn from time to time during the rolling. This will prevent the dough sticking to the surface, and will help keep the thickness even.

3 ▲ Continue rolling out until the dough circle is about 2 in (5 cm) larger all round than the tin. The dough will be about ⅛ in (3 mm) thick.

4 ▲ Set the rolling pin on the dough, near one side of the circle. Fold the outside edge of dough over the pin, then roll the pin over the dough to wrap the dough round it. Do this gently and loosely.

5 ▲ Hold the pin over the tin and gently unroll the dough so it drapes into the tin, centring it as much as possible.

6 ▲ With your fingertips, lift and ease the dough into the tin, gently pressing it over the bottom and up the side. Turn excess dough over the rim and trim it with a knife or scissors, depending on the edge to be made.

FINISHING THE EDGE

1 ▲ For a forked edge: Trim the dough even with the rim and press it flat. Firmly and evenly press the prongs of a fork all round the edge. If the fork sticks, dip it in flour.

Apple and Cherry Crumble Pie
Mix together 12 oz (340 g) peeled, cored and sliced Granny Smith apples, 10 oz (300 g) stoned cherries and 4 oz (115 g) soft light brown sugar. Put into a 9 in (23 cm) pastry case. For the topping, combine 4 oz (115 g) plain flour, 4 oz (115 g) soft light brown sugar and 1 teaspoon ground cinnamon. Rub in 3 oz (85 g) butter until the mixture resembles coarse crumbs. Sprinkle over the fruit. Bake in a 375°F/190°C/Gas 5 oven for about 45 minutes or until golden. *Serves 6.*

2 ▲ For a crimped edge: Trim the dough to leave an overhang of about ½ in (1.5 cm) all round. Fold the extra dough under. Put the knuckle or tip of the index finger of one of your hands inside the edge, pointing directly out. With the thumb and index finger of your other hand, pinch the dough edge around your index finger into a 'V' shape. Continue all round the edge.

4 ▲ For a cutout edge: Trim the dough even with the rim and press it flat on the rim. With a small pastry cutter, cut out decorative shapes from the dough trimmings. Moisten the edge of the pastry case and press the cutouts in place, overlapping them slightly if you like.

3 ▲ For a ruffled edge: Trim the dough to leave an overhang of about ½ in (1.5 cm) all round. Fold the extra dough under. Hold the thumb and index finger of one of your hands about 1 in (2.5 cm) apart, inside the edge, pointing directly out. With the index finger of your other hand, gently pull the dough between them, to the end of the rim. Continue all the way round the edge.

5 ▲ For a ribbon edge: Trim the dough even with the rim and press it flat on the rim. Cut long strips about ¾ in (2 cm) wide from the dough trimmings. Moisten the edge and press one end of a strip on to it. Twist the strip gently and press it on to the edge again. Continue all the way round the edge.

MAKING A TWO-CRUST PIE

Two succulent pastry layers enveloping a sweet filling – what could be nicer? Use the same method for making small pies, such as mince pices.

American-style Apple Pie
Combine 2 lb (900 g) peeled, cored and thinly sliced Granny Smith apples, 1 tablespoon plain flour, 3½ oz (100 g) caster sugar and ¾ teaspoon mixed spice. Toss to coat the fruit evenly with the sugar and flour. Use to fill the two-crust pie. Bake in a 375°F/190°C/ Gas 5 oven for about 45 minutes or until the pastry is golden brown and the fruit is tender (test with a skewer through a slit in the top crust). Cool on a rack.

1 ▲ Roll out half of the pastry dough on a floured surface and line a pie tin that is about 2 in (5 cm) deep. Trim the dough even with the rim.

3 ▲ Roll out a second piece of dough to a circle that is about 1 in (2.5 cm) larger all round than the tin. Roll it up around the rolling pin and unroll over the pie. Press the edges together.

2 ▲ Put in the filling. Brush the edge of the pastry case evenly with water to moisten it.

4 ▲ Trim the edge of the lid to leave a ½ in (1.5 cm) overhang. Cut slits or a design in the centre. These will act as steam vents during baking.

5 ▲ Fold the overhang of the lid under the edge of the case. Press the two together gently and evenly to seal. Finish the edge as wished.

6 ▲ Brush the top of the pie with milk or cream for a shiny finish. Or brush with 1 egg yolk mixed with 1 teaspoon water for a glazed golden brown finish. Or brush with water and then sprinkle with caster sugar or cinnamon and sugar for a sugary crust.

7 ▲ If you like, cut out decorative shapes from the dough trimmings, rolled out as thinly as possible. Moisten the cutouts with a little water and press them on to the top. Glaze the decorations before baking.

MAKING A LATTICE TOP

A woven pastry lattice is a very attractive finish for a pie. Prepare shortcrust for a two-crust pie.

Roll out half of the pastry dough and line the pie tin. Trim the dough to leave a ½ in (1.5 cm) overhang all round. Put in the filling. Roll out the second piece of dough into a circle that is about 2 in (5 cm) larger all round than the pie tin.

1 ▲ With the help of a ruler, cut neat straight strips of dough that are about ½ in (1.5 cm) wide, using a knife or fluted pastry wheel.

2 ▲ For a square woven lattice: Lay half of the strips across the pie filling, keeping them neatly parallel and spacing them evenly.

Apricot Lattice Pie
Toss together 2¼ lb (1 kg) peeled, stoned and thinly sliced apricots, 2 tablespoons plain flour and 3½ oz (100 g) sugar. Fill the pastry case and make a lattice top. Glaze with milk and bake in a 375°F/190°C/Gas 5 oven for about 45 minutes or until the pastry is golden and the filling is bubbling. Cool on a wire rack.

3 ▲ Fold back every other strip from the centre. Lay another strip across the centre, on the flat strips, at right angles to them. Lay the folded strips flat again.

4 ▲ Now fold back those strips that were not folded the first time. Lay another strip across those that are flat now, spacing this new strip evenly from the centre strip.

5 ▲ Continue folding the strips in this way until half of the lattice is completed. Repeat on the other half of the pie.

6 ▲ Trim the ends of the strips even with the rim of the pie tin. Moisten the edge of the pastry case and press the strips gently to it to seal. Finish the edge.

7 ▲ For a diamond lattice: Weave as above, laying the intersecting strips diagonally instead of at right angles. Or lay half the strips over the filling and the remaining strips on top.

LINING A FLAN TIN OR RING

A flan tin is shallow, with no rim. Its straight sides (smooth or fluted) give a tart or flan the traditional shape. The most useful tins have removable bases, making it very easy to turn out a tart. Flan rings are straight-sided metal rings that are set on a baking sheet.

In addition to flan tins and rings, there are porcelain quiche dishes and small, individual tartlet tins, both plain and fluted.

Pecan Nut Tartlets
Line six 4 in (10 cm) tartlet tins with flan pastry. Place 1 oz (30 g) pecan nut halves in each. In a bowl, beat 3 eggs to mix. Add 1 oz (30 g) melted butter, 10 oz (300 g) golden syrup and ½ teaspoon vanilla essence. Sift together 4 oz (115 g) caster sugar and 1 tablespoon plain flour. Add to the egg mixture and stir until evenly blended. Fill the tartlet cases and leave until the nuts rise to the surface. Bake in a 350°F/ 180°C/Gas 4 oven for 35–40 minutes or until a knife inserted near the centre comes out clean. Cool in the tins for 15 minutes, then turn on to a wire rack.

1 ▲ Remove the chilled dough from the refrigerator and let it soften slightly at room temperature. Roll out to a circle about 2 in (5 cm) larger all round than the tin or ring. It will be about ⅛ in (3 mm) thick.

2 ▲ Roll up the dough round the rolling pin, then unroll it over the tin or ring, draping it gently.

3 ▲ With your fingertips, ease the dough into the tin or ring, gently pressing it smoothly over the bottom, without stretching it.

4 ▲ Fold the overhanging dough down inside the tin or ring, to thicken the side of the pastry case. Smooth and press the side of the case against the side of the tin or ring.

5 ▲ Roll the rolling pin over the top of the tin or ring to cut off excess dough. Smooth the cut edge and press it against the side of the tin or ring, if necessary, to keep it in place.

6 ▲ **For tartlet tins:** Arrange them close together and unroll the dough over them, draping it loosely. Roll the rolling pin over the top to cut off excess pastry. Press into the bottom and sides of the tins.

BAKING BLIND

Baked custard and cream fillings can make pastry soggy, so the cases for these flans and tarts are often given an initial baking before the filling is added and the final baking is done. Such pre-baking is referred to as baking 'blind'. The technique is also used for pastry cases that are to be filled with an uncooked or precooked mixture.

The purpose of using weights is to prevent the bottom of the pastry case from rising too much and becoming distorted, thus keeping its neat shape.

Fresh Strawberry Flan
Make the case using sweet flan pastry or rich sweet flan pastry. Bake it blind fully, then allow to cool. Beat 14 oz (400 g) full-fat soft cheese with 1¾ oz (50 g) caster sugar, 1 egg yolk and 4 table-spoons whipping cream until the mixture is smooth. Fold in 1 stiffly whisked egg white. Pour into the case and spread evenly. Bake at 350°F/180°C/Gas 4 for 15–20 minutes or until the filling is softly set; it will set further as it cools. When cool, arrange halved strawberries on top of the flan in concentric circles. Melt 5 oz (145 g) red-currant jelly and brush over the berries to glaze them. Leave to cool before serving. *Serves 6.*

1 ▲ Set the pie or flan tin, or flan ring, on a sheet of greaseproof paper or foil. Draw or mark around its base. Cut out a circle about 3 in (7.5 cm) larger all round than the drawn or marked one.

3 ▲ Lay the circle of greaseproof paper or foil in the pastry case and press it smoothly over the bottom and up the side.

5 ▲ **For partially baked pastry:** Bake the case in a 400°F/200°C/Gas 6 oven for 15–20 minutes or until it is slightly dry and set. Remove the paper or foil and beans. The pastry is now ready to be filled and baked further.

2 ▲ Roll out the pastry dough and use to line the tin or ring set on a baking sheet. Prick the bottom of the pastry case all over with a fork.

4 ▲ Put enough dried beans or baking beans in the case to cover the bottom thickly.

6 ▲ **For fully baked pastry:** After baking for 15 minutes, remove the paper or foil and beans. Prick the bottom again with a fork. Return to the oven and bake for 5–10 minutes or until golden brown. Cool completely before adding the filling.

MAKING CHOUX PASTRY

Unlike other pastries, where the fat is rubbed into the flour, with choux pastry the butter is melted with water and then the flour is added, followed by eggs. The result is more of a paste than a pastry. It is easy to make, but care must be taken in measuring the ingredients.

FOR 18 PROFITEROLES OR 12 ECLAIRS

4 oz (115 g) butter, cut into small pieces
8 fl oz (240 ml) water
2 teaspoons caster sugar (optional)
¼ teaspoon salt
5 oz (145 g) plain flour
4 eggs, beaten to mix

Shaping choux pastry
- For *large puffs*: Use two large spoons dipped in water. Drop the paste in 2–2½ in (5–6 cm) wide blobs on the paper-lined baking sheet, leaving 1½ in (4 cm) between each. Neaten the blobs as much as possible. Alternatively, for well-shaped puffs, pipe the paste using a piping bag fitted with a ¾ in (2 cm) plain nozzle.
- For *profiteroles*: Use two small spoons or a piping bag fitted with a ½ in (1.5 cm) nozzle and shape 1 in (2.5 cm) blobs.
- For *éclairs*: Use a piping bag fitted with a ¾ in (2 cm) nozzle. Pipe strips 4–5 in (10–12 cm) long.
- For *a ring*: draw a 12 in (30 cm) circle on the paper. Spoon the paste in large blobs on the circle to make a ring. Or pipe two rings round the circle and a third on top.

Baking times for choux pastry
Bake large puffs and éclairs 30–35 minutes, profiteroles 20–25 minutes, rings 40–45 minutes.

1 ▲ Combine the butter, water, sugar, if using, and salt in a large heavy-based saucepan. Bring to the boil over moderately high heat, stirring occasionally.

3 ▲ Return the pan to moderate heat and cook, stirring, until the mixture will form a ball, pulling away from the side of the pan. This will take about 1 minute. Remove from the heat again and allow to cool for 3–5 minutes.

5 ▲ While still warm, shape large choux puffs, éclairs, profiteroles or large rings on a baking sheet lined with baking parchment.

2 ▲ As soon as the mixture is boiling, remove the pan from the heat. Add the flour all at once and beat vigorously with a wooden spoon to mix the flour into the liquid.

4 ▲ Add a little of the beaten egg and beat well with the spoon or an electric mixer to incorporate. Add a little more egg and beat in well. Continue beating in the eggs until the mixture becomes a smooth, shiny paste thick enough to hold its shape.

6 ▲ Glaze with 1 egg beaten with 1 teaspoon cold water. Put into a 425°F/220°C/Gas 7 oven, then reduce the heat to 400°F/200°C/Gas 6. Bake until puffed and golden brown.

7 ▶ When baked (see baking times, left) use the tip of a knife to make a slit in the side of each puff or éclair, or several around a ring, to let the steam inside escape. Return to the turned-off oven and dry out for 5–10 minutes. Cool on a wire rack. Shortly before serving, split the pastries open horizontally and fill as desired.

Fillings for choux pastry
● Fill sweet choux pastry with sweetened whipped cream, vanilla ice cream or sweetened chestnut purée. Serve it with bittersweet chocolate sauce.
● Fill savoury choux with cheese sauce or creamed chicken.

Hot Cheddar Puffs

MAKES ABOUT 28 APPETIZER PUFFS

2 oz (55 g) butter, cut into pieces

8 fl oz (240 ml) water

½ teaspoon salt

5 oz (145 g) plain flour

¼ teaspoon mustard powder

good pinch of hot paprika

2 oz (55 g) mature Cheddar cheese, grated

4 eggs, beaten

1 egg beaten with 1 teaspoon cold water, to glaze

FOR THE FILLING

8 oz (225 g) full-fat soft cheese, at room temperature

2 tablespoons spicy fruit sauce

4 tablespoons diced canned pimiento

2 tablespoons chopped black olives

1 Preheat a 425°F/220°C/Gas 7 oven.

2 Make the choux pastry, adding the mustard and paprika with the flour and beating in the cheese before the eggs. Shape into small puffs on a baking sheet lined with baking parchment. Brush with the egg glaze.

3 Put in the oven and reduce the temperature to 400°F/200°C/Gas 6. Bake for 20–25 minutes or until risen, golden brown and crisp.

4 ▲ Meanwhile, for the filling, beat the soft cheese with the spicy fruit sauce until well blended. Mix in the pimiento and olives.

5 Cut a slit in the side of each puff and return to the turned-off oven to dry out for about 10 minutes.

6 ▼ While the puffs are still warm, fill them with the cheese filling, piping or spooning it carefully into the slit cut in the side of each puff. Serve the Cheddar puffs warm.

Index

~

A

American frosting, 107
American-style apple pie, 120
apples
  American-style apple pie, 120
  apple and cherry crumble pie, 119
  boned pork loin with apple
    cream sauce, 19
  cutting, 92
  pork and apple batter
    puddings, 86
  preparing, 90, 91
apricots
  apricot lattice pie, 121
  cutting, 93
  preparing, 90
  stoning, 91
aubergines
  preparing and cooking, 63
avocados
  cutting, 93
  preparing, 90, 92

B

bacon
  country chicken sauté, 16
  fisherman's stew, 44
baking
  eggs, 81
  fish, 34
  rice, 54
baking tins, 6
bananas
  banana bread, 103
  banana walnut bread, 103
  bananas baked with rum, 93
  cutting, 93
  preparing, 90
batter
  making, 86
  pork and apple batter
    puddings, 86
beans
  preparing, 56
  types of, 56
beef
  beef stew with dumplings, 25
  rib of beef with shallots, 22
  stir-fried beef with mange-tout, 28
berry sauce, 98
black beans, 56
black-eye beans, 56
blackcurrants
  preparing, 91
boiling eggs, 78
boned pork loin with apple cream
  sauce, 19
braising, 21
bread
  bowknot rolls, 105
  crescent rolls, 105
  everyday white bread, 104
  Parker House rolls, 105
  rolls, shaping, 105

broccoli
  broccoli, cauliflower and carrot
    salad, 69
  preparing and cooking, 65
Brussels sprouts
  preparing and cooking, 67
bulgar wheat
  bulgar wheat salad with herbs, 57
  preparing, 57
  simple bulgar pilaf, 57
buttered noodles, 48

C

cabbage
  preparing and cooking, 66
cake tins, 6, 110
cakes
  all-in-one method, 108
  buttercream, 108
  chocolate fairy cakes, 109
  chocolate ice cream roll, 113
  classic whisked sponge, 112
  creaming method, 106
  Genoese sponge, 111
  mocha Victoria sponge, 106
  Swiss roll, 113
  Victoria sandwich, 106
  whisked sponge, using separated
    eggs for, 111
canned food, storing, 8
carambola
  cutting, 93
  preparing, 90
  slicing, 92
carrots
  broccoli, cauliflower and carrot
    salad, 69
  carrot purée, 71
  preparing and cooking, 60
carving
  poultry, 13
casseroles and stews
  beef stew with dumplings, 25
  fisherman's stew, 44
  stewing with a fry start, 24
cauliflower
  broccoli, cauliflower and carrot
    salad, 69
  cauliflower cheese, 66
  preparing and cooking, 66
celeriac
  preparing and cooking, 62
celery
  preparing and cooking, 67
cheese
  cauliflower cheese, 66
  cheese and herb dip, 68
  hot Cheddar puffs, 125
  lettuce with blue cheese
    dressing, 75
  ricotta and peach pancakes, 87
cherries
  apple and cherry crumble
    pie, 119
  stoning, 91

chicken
  country chicken sauté, 16
  frying, 17
  simple roast chicken, 12
  succulent fried chicken, 17
chicory
  preparing, 74
chocolate
  chocolate buttercream, 108
  chocolate custard, 85
  chocolate fairy cakes, 109
  chocolate ice cream roll, 113
choux pastry
  baking, 124
  fillings, 125
  hot Cheddar puffs, 125
  making, 124
  shaping, 124
citrus fruit
  cutting, 93
  garnishes, 94
  preparing, 90, 91
clams
  lemon pasta with clam sauce, 51
  preparing, 41
country chicken sauté, 16
courgettes
  pasta with courgette and walnut
    sauce, 70
  preparing and cooking, 63
crunchy muesli muffins, 102
custard
  chocolate, 85
  liqueur, 85
  making, 85
  mocha, 85
  orange, 85
  variations, 85

D

dates
  preparing, 91
deep-fried catfish, 40
dip
  cheese and herb dip, 68

E

éclairs, 124
eggs,
  baking, 81
  boiling, 78
  caviar-crowned eggs, 78
  coddled, 78
  egg, potato and bean salad, 78
  fried eggs and sausage on
    tortillas, 80
  frying, 80
  hard-boiled, 78
  poached eggs Florentine, 82
  poaching, 82
  rolled omelette, 84
  scrambled eggs with smoked
    salmon, 79
  scrambling, 79

smoked salmon eggs, 78
whisked sponge, using separated
  eggs for, 111
endive
  preparing, 74
equipment, 6, 7

F

fish
  baked fish steaks, 34
  baking, 34
  coating and frying, 40
  cutlets, 33
  deep-fried catfish, 40
  determining when cooked, 35
  escalope, 33
  fillet, 33
  fillets, cutting, 38
  fish kebabs with lemon butter, 39
  fisherman's stew, 44
  frying, 40
  grilling, 39
  gutted, 33
  poaching, 36
  steak, 33
  steaks and cutlets,
    cutting, 37
  steaming, 37
  stock, 44
  types of, 32, 34, 35
  whole, preparing for cooking, 32
flans
  fresh strawberry flan, 123
  tin or ring, lining, 122
French beans
  egg, potato and bean salad, 78
frosting
  American, 107
  lemon, 107
  orange, 107
fruit
  berry sauce, 98
  citrus, 90, 91
  coulis, 98
  cutting, 92, 93
  fresh colour, keeping, 92
  fresh, preparing, 90–3
  storing, 7
fruit ices, 97
frying
  eggs, 80
  fish, 40
  poultry, 17

G

garlic
  chopping, 68
  whole, peeling, 68
Genoese sponge, 111
gooseberries
  preparing, 92
grapes
  preparing, 92
gravy, 22

H

ham
  pasta with ham and peas, 50
  scallops wrapped in Parma
    ham, 43
haricot beans, 56
herbs
  bulgar wheat salad with herbs, 57
  cheese and herb dip, 68
  chopping, 68
  fresh herb pasta, 49
  herb and garlic pasta, 49
  melon salad with herbs, 95
  pot-roast veal with herbs, 26
  steamed salmon with herbs, 37
  vegetable and herb chowder, 72
hot Cheddar puffs, 125

I

ice cream
  chocolate ice cream roll, 113
iced macaroon cream with
    raspberry sauce, 98
icing
  American frosting, 107

J

jointing poultry, 14

K

kebabs
  fish kebabs with lemon butter, 39
kidney beans, 56
kiwi fruit
  cutting, 93
  preparing, 90
knives, 6

L

lamb
  roast leg of lamb, 20
lamb's lettuce
  preparing, 74
lasagne
  tuna lasagne, 52
leeks
  preparing and cooking, 62
lemons
  lemon buttercream, 108
  lemon frosting, 107
  lemon pasta, 49
  lemon pasta with clam sauce, 51
lentils, 56
lettuce
  lettuce with blue cheese
    dressing, 75
  preparing, 74
liqueur custard, 85
lychees
  preparing, 90

M

macaroons
  iced macaroon cream with
    raspberry sauce, 98

mange-tout
  stir-fried beef with mange-
    tout, 28
mangoes
  preparing, 90
  stoning, 91
measuring
  dry ingredients, 9
  liquid ingredients, 9
meat
  barding, 18
  braising, 21
  browning, 26
  chining, 18
  cooking methods, 21
  cuts, choice of, 21
  determining when cooked, 21
  grilling, 21
  pan-frying, 21, 27
  pot-roasting, 21, 26
  preparing for cooking, 18
  roasting, 20, 21
  sautéing, 27
  searing, 26
  stewing, 21, 24
  stir-frying, 21, 28
  stock, 29
  testing, 21
melon
  basket, 95
  cutting, 93
  melon salad with herbs, 95
  preparing, 91, 94
mixing bowls, 7
mocha
  mocha buttercream, 108
  mocha custard, 85
  mocha Victoria sponge, 106
muesli
  crunchy muesli muffins, 102
muffins
  crunchy muesli muffins, 102
  making, 102
mushrooms
  country chicken sauté, 16
  preparing and cooking, 67
mussels
  preparing, 41
  sailor's mussels, 41

N

nectarines
  cutting, 93
  stoning, 91
noodles
  buttered noodles, 48
nut shortcrust pastry, 116

O

omelettes
  ideas for, 84
  rolled, 84
onions
  chopping, 68
  preparing and cooking, 62
oranges
  orange buttercream, 108
  orange custard, 85
  orange frosting, 107

P

pan-fried Teriyaki steak, 27
pan-fried trout with olives and
    capers, 33
pan-frying, 21, 27
pancakes
  making, 87
  ricotta and peach pancakes, 87
papayas
  cutting, 93
  preparing, 90
  seeding, 91
Parker House rolls, 105
Parma ham
  scallops wrapped in Parma ham, 43
parsnips
  preparing and cooking, 60
passion fruit
  preparing, 90
pasta
  cooking, 48
  dough, making, 49
  drying, 51
  flat shapes, 52
  flavourings, 49
  fresh herb, 49
  green, 49
  herb and garlic, 49
  lemon, 49
  lemon pasta with clam sauce, 51
  machine, using, 51
  pasta with courgette and walnut
    sauce, 70
  pasta with ham and peas, 50
  rolling and cutting dough by
    hand, 50
  saffron, 49
  storage, 50
  tomato, 49
  tuna lasagne, 52
  wholemeal, 49
pastry
  baking blind, 123
  choux, 124
  edge, finishing, 119
  flat tin or ring, lining, 122
  French flan, 117
  lattice top, 121
  rich flan, 117
  rich sweet flan, 117
  rolling out, 118
  shortcrust, 116
  sweet flan, 117
  tin, lining, 118
  two-crust pie, 116, 120
peaches
  cutting, 93
  preparing, 90
  ricotta and peach pancakes, 87
  stoning, 91
pears
  cutting, 92
  preparing, 90, 91
peas
  dried, 56
  pasta with ham and peas, 50
  preparing and cooking, 65
pecan nut tartlets, 122
pies
  American-style apple pie, 120

apple and cherry crumble
    pie, 119
apricot lattice pie, 121
two-crust, 116, 120
pineapple
  cutting, 93
  preparing, 90, 92, 96
  tipsy pineapple boat, 96
  wedges, 96
pinto beans, 56
plums
  cutting, 93
  stoning, 91
poached eggs Florentine, 82
poached sole fillets, 36
poaching
  eggs, 82
  fish, 36
pomegranates
  preparing, 90
pork
  boned pork loin with apple
    cream sauce, 19
  fried eggs and sausage on
    tortillas, 80
  pork and apple batter
    puddings, 86
pot-roast veal with herbs, 26
pot-roasting, 21, 26
potatoes
  egg, potato and bean salad, 78
  mashing, 71
  preparing and cooking, 61
  stuffed jacket-baked potatoes, 61
poultry
  carving, 13
  frying, 17
  jointing, 15
  raw, handling, 15
  roasting, 12
  sautés, 16
  stuffing, 14
  trussing, 14
poussins Waldorf, 13
prawns
  deveining, 42
  peeling, 42
  spicy butterflied tiger prawns, 42
preparation tools, 7
profiteroles, 124
pulses
  preparing, 56
  types of, 56
pumpkins
  preparing, 63

Q

quinces
  cutting, 92
  preparing, 90, 91

R

raspberries
  iced macaroon cream with
    raspberry sauce, 98
redcurrants
  preparing, 91
rhubarb
  preparing, 90

rib of beef with shallots, 22
rice
  baking, 54
  cooking, 54
  long-grain, 54
  medium-grain, 54
  rice salad, 54
  sautéing, 54
  short-grain, 54
  steaming, 54
  varieties of, 54
  wild, cooking, 55
  wild rice and turkey salad, 55
rich flan pastry, 117
rich shortcrust pastry, 116
rich sweet flan pastry, 117
ricotta and peach pancakes, 87
roast leg of lamb, 20
roasting
  meat, 20, 21
  poultry, 12
roasting tins, 6
rocket
  preparing, 74

S
saffron pasta, 49
sailor's mussels, 41
salads
  broccoli, cauliflower and carrot
    salad, 69
  bulgar wheat salad with herbs, 57
  egg, potato and bean salad, 78
  lettuce with blue cheese
    dressing, 75
  melon salad with herbs, 95
  rice salad, 54
  wild rice and turkey salad, 54
salad dressing
  blue cheese dressing, 75
salad greens
  preparing, 74

rinsing and crisping, 75
salmon
  steamed salmon with herbs, 37
saucepans, 6
sauces
  berry, 98
  deglazing for, 27
  pasta with courgette and
    walnut sauce, 70
sautéing
  meat, 27
  poultry, 16
  rice, 54
scallops
  preparing, 43
  scallops wrapped in Parma
    ham, 43
searing meat, 26
shallots
  rib of beef with shallots, 22
shortcrust pastry, 116
simple roast chicken, 12
smoked salmon
  scrambled eggs with smoked
    salmon, 79
  smoked salmon eggs, 78
sole
  poached sole fillets, 36
sorbets, 97
soups
  vegetable and herb
    chowder, 72
spices, 8
spicy butterflied tiger prawns, 42
spinach
  poached eggs Florentine, 82
  preparing and cooking, 64
star fruit
  preparing, 90, 92, 93
steak
  pan-fried Teriyaki steak, 27
  testing, 27
steamed salmon with herbs, 37

steaming
  fish, 37
  rice, 54
stewing, 21
stews see casseroles
stir-fried beef with mange-tout, 28
stir-frying, 21, 28
stock
  fish, 44
  meat, 29
  vegetable, 72
storing food, 7, 8
strawberries
  fresh strawberry flan, 123
  preparing, 92
  strawberry ice, 97
stuffing poultry, 14
stuffing tips, 14
succulent fried chicken, 17
swede
  cooking, 61
  preparing, 61
sweet flan pastry, 117
sweet potatoes
  mashing, 71
  sweet potato purée, 71
Swiss roll, 113

T
teabreads
  banana bread, 103
  banana walnut bread, 103
  making, 102
timing, 8
tortillas
  fried eggs and sausage on
    tortillas, 80
trout
  pan-fried trout with olives and
    capers, 33
trussing poultry, 14
tuna lasagne, 52

turkey
  wild rice and turkey salad, 54

V
veal
  pot-roast veal with herbs, 26
vegetables
  blanching and refreshing, 69
  chopping, 68
  mashing, 71
  preparing and cooking, 60–7
  puréeing, 71
  stock, 72
  storing, 7
  stuffed jacket-baked potatoes, 61
  sweating, 70
  vegetable and herb chowder, 72
Victoria sandwich, 106

W
walnuts
  banana walnut bread, 103
  pasta with courgette and walnut
    sauce, 70
watercress
  preparing, 74
watermelon
  preparing, 92
  watermelon basket, 94
wheat, bulgar see bulgar wheat
wholemeal pasta, 49
wild rice
  cooking, 55
  wild rice and turkey salad, 55

Y
yeast dough
  everyday white bread, 104
  making, 104
  rolls, 105